William Klein

William Klein

Introduction by Christian Caujolle

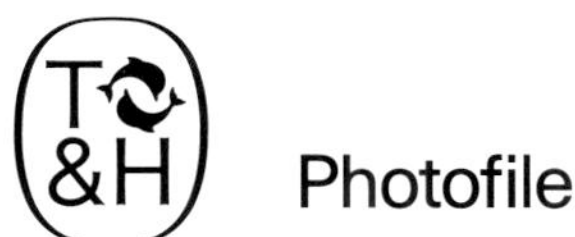

Photofile

The Photofile series is the original English-language edition of the Photo Poche collection. It was first published between 1986 and 1992 by the Centre National de la Photographie, Paris, with the support of the French Ministry of Culture. Robert Delpire (1926–2017) was the creator of the series and its managing editor until 2017.

To Jeanine and Pierre.

The photographs reproduced in this book
were taken with Leica M and R cameras.

General editor: Géraldine Lay
Series design by Matthew Young

Translated from the French

First published in the United Kingdom in 2017 by
Thames & Hudson Ltd, 181A High Holborn, London WC1V 7QX

First published in the United States of America in 2017 by
Thames & Hudson Inc., 500 Fifth Avenue, New York, New York 10110

British Library Cataloguing-in-Publication Data
A catalogue record for this book is available from the British Library

Library of Congress Control Number 2016941852

ISBN 978-0-500-41112-4

Printed and bound in Italy

The chance witness

Trance witness revels

The full title of my New York book is Life is Good & Good for You in New York William Klein trance witness revels. I believe that these last three words sum up how I see photography. To me, the act of taking a photograph is a moment of trance in which you can capture many hundreds of things happening at the same time and through which you can feel them and see them, consciously or not.

William Klein

The mystery of an eye

But there is something else that I have experienced many times when I have had the privilege to sit at a cutting table and edit William Klein's film material. I stop by chance at a single frame, demonstrators in Paris in May 1968 or New Yorkers walking the streets, and what I see is a Klein photograph, with the same apparent disorder, the same glut of information, gestures and looks pointing in all directions, and yet at the same time governed by an organized, rigorous perspective.... We are faced by the mystery of an eye that instinctively cuts reality into slices of Klein, just as Van Gogh cut it into slices of Van Gogh....

Chris Marker

Strange things

Some photographers see strange things. Or more precisely, they see things in a strange way; gun-toting children on the streets of New York, elegant ladies smoking three cigarettes at the same time, a Japanese artist who seems to be painting with his entire body, models wearing haute couture alongside waxworks of Napoleon and Josephine. All of these things have been seen by William Klein. An apparently divisive figure, who has been the subject of more than one controversy, creating surprise and confusion as he jumps

from painting to photography, from filmmaking to graphic design
and back again. A photographer whose images have been called too
dark, too packed, too messy, too much. A photographer who, despite
the small world of photography's love of labels, has often been
considered unclassifiable. It has often been asked why this man, who
is still regularly called an *enfant terrible*, likes to cram so many people
and objects into his images. One quite serious explanation could
be suggested: Klein uses his camera shutter to capture dense and
complicated situations and store them away so that he can pore over
them later in greater detail, as contact sheets or prints. Ultimately,
however, photographers remain solitary figures and it is hard to move
beyond their disarming surfaces, but a pragmatic approach may yet
give us some clues.

Eyewitness accounts

In August 1983, close to the Grotto of Massabielle in Lourdes, which
was about to receive an official visit from Pope John Paul II, William
Klein was taking pictures. Like the rest of his colleagues, he was
obliged to stand in line to obtain an official pass; he was there on
behalf of *Libération* – just a newspaper photographer, whose rolls of
film were taken away as soon as he'd finished shooting, with no choice
of his own, waiting for the morning paper to see what was left of
his work. Once I saw him in front of a procession of Poles who had
arrived for the occasion, letting them come towards him with his Leica
glued to his eye. He hardly moved, the two rows of pilgrims flowing
past him as if he wasn't there, while he kept shooting at point-blank
range. Too obvious and too present to be awkward. He disappeared
into a multiform and melancholy crowd where odd figures clad in
transparent plastic took out novelty containers shaped like the Virgin
Mary and filled them with holy water; he followed the blazing votive
candles, the gathered invalids, the surging masses who were both
sheeplike and ecstatic, wandered through the museum that tells the
tale of the Lourdes miracle in waxworks, captured the miraculous
baths where photography is forbidden, and clothed the evening
pilgrims in light from his camera flash. This crowd, like the many
other crowds he has collected, seeking to bring order to chaos within

each shot, was simply a pretext to take images of anxiety. He was an iconoclast in a land of holy images.

A few months later, I saw William Klein again in another crowd, choosing images from his freshly developed contact sheets, which he had shot at the huge 'Free School' demonstrations happening in Paris. He was talking to himself and making marks in red pencil, apparently amazed to find on paper the mass of faces that had driven him to press the shutter release, the swarming throng in front of the lens that he had caught within a frame, to pass on to us. Once again, he had encountered enigmatic faces, like those in paintings by Pieter Bruegel the Elder, whose details seem to sum up an entire society. With his sense of tragedy and his blackly comic New York Jewish sense of humour, he saw himself as many things at once: a news reporter, a paparazzo from one of the papers of his youth, and a walking photo booth.

A sense of flux

Where does this sense of flux come from, the one that emanates from these photographs? It's hard to explain. We could seek a technical explanation for it. To Klein, the act of photography is both physical and cultural. Photography to him is a discharge of energy, sensual and violent. It is from this that the overturning of traditional concepts of framing and the introduction of elements such as chance, distortion and motion all spring. After having shifted geometry, Klein was the first to introduce the shiver of life that motion brings into street photography.

Alain Jouffroy, I grandi fotografi, 1983

Klein and the establishment

When he became one of the few photographers to be honoured with an exhibition at the Centre Pompidou, William Klein did not want to fill the walls with signed and framed prints of the kind that museums and the art market love so much. He imagined a slideshow, made up of three screens on which would be shown a parade of his images, both famous and previously unpublished, ranging from fashion to portraits, from Rome to Tokyo, from his own street corner to a wide selection of commissions. Nearby TV screens showed extracts from his films, rushes from his ad campaigns and a slow scan over a long series of contact sheets. A photography exhibition in which material presence was replaced by a staging that was both cryptic and sumptuous. It is also worth remembering that William Klein took pictures in order to make books. He once gave up photography because he thought he could find something better to do, and was tired of failing to create the dialogue he wanted from his pictures; he lets his passions of the moment carry him along; he never goes out without a camera, sometimes even taking it to his own street corner; he seems to do everything on impulse; he is unusually professional and precise, as demanding as he ought to be and as anticonformist as he needs to be; he loves what he does and hates it when what he wanted to show is betrayed. In short, this scrupulous jack-of-all-trades is, as those in his field have often been, a difficult customer. It is also worth remembering that he doesn't like it when his pictures are sabotaged with deep, tar-like blacks; he argued with Aperture, the respected photography publisher, when they would not admit that his book had been poorly printed; he has made films and even commercials; he has strong ideas about page layouts; he has been an inspiration to many – who often jump to his defence – with his use of the wide-angle lens and the flash at a time when those things were out of style; he has never belonged to any school, agency or movement; he never does anything he doesn't want to do. Add all these things together and you have a portrait of the kind of person guaranteed to exasperate the photographic establishment.

It should also be added that Klein has never taken all that many photographs and that the time he has spent working with still images has lessened as the years have gone by. Formerly he would spend two uninterrupted months taking pictures to turn into a book, followed by another four to see the project through to its end. Nowadays he rarely spends more than two or three days in a row taking pictures, whenever the need is there.

A few observations

In the 1950s, many photographers saw the young Bill Klein as a potential troublemaker. This was the era of reportage. It was believed that photographers were meant to record the 'Family of Man' and thus allow us to discover the world – the real world – through their images. Fashion favoured 'clean' photography, polished compositions, rules inherited from the fine arts. But Klein went out into the streets to move around with the people there, face to face, letting the city and the streets surprise him. He was an outsider, not 'clean' at all. He hadn't forgotten that not long before, after leaving the studio of Fernand Léger, he put together a maquette of abstract images created in a darkroom by moving cardboard squares, circles and triangles across photosensitive paper: the theme of motion brought together with the issues of time and form. Klein found that many people didn't like his images that showed Americans a version of New York that was too 'dark', its streets packed with signposts, violent motion and mocking games in front of the camera. New York, Moscow, Rome, Tokyo: all of these cities became books with pioneering designs that still remain striking today – urban short stories. The same period also brought a contract from *Vogue*, at the same time as Robert Frank. It would later be said, yoking the two men together with disarming ease, that this pair of photographers changed photography in the fifties. This ignored the fact that Klein coped with the changing world by building a new grammar out of chaos and plenty, while the impressionistic Frank projected the cultural confusion of a lone European upon an America in which he was an immigrant. But this comparison is unimportant and perhaps even meaningless, except as a way of reconstructing chronological history.

Given these facts, it is easy to see why a museum curator might say that Klein's images were difficult to understand, that this was the case when he took them and that they would remain so, and that consequently his photographic career would clearly be short-lived. Of course, anyone can make a mistake, especially regarding somebody who has spent almost twenty years focusing more heavily on filmmaking and politics, who has always remained outside of cliques and who does not show people the shots he takes only for himself, when he feels the urge, rather than for exhibitions. But today, when young people who've once again begun to dream of changing the world are naively pointing their cameras all over the place, it's hard not to notice that Klein has already broken all of those rules, just by following his own heart. Think of those images full of bodies and faces sliced up by the edge of the frame, showing you a world so packed and swarming it may as well be a Marx Brothers movie. And yet, how many times has one of Klein's photographs, and the violence of its approach, demanded your attention and forced you to read it? Surely far more often than most exercises in composition, and surely because it says more in a shorter space of time.

Cosmopolitan visions

It's interesting to make the obvious comparison between Klein and Weegee, who had a comparable stake in a squalid New York and who really was from the News. Linking them like this, one sees immediately that — aside from the similarity of their supreme voyeurist chutzpah — one was a primitive putting on airs, while the other was a modernist slumming with jazzy abandon. There is hardly anything like the real-life murder-and-mayhem of the journalist in Klein (only toy guns and charades of violence), and there is nothing of Klein's extreme artistic rawness visually decomposing before your eyes in Weegee. This is not simply the difference between parochial spirit and cosmopolitan vision. The real contrast emerges in their attitudes toward the media, which both exploited, but for opposite reasons.

That to which Weegee frustratedly aspired, the status of artist, was the easiest thing for Klein to shuck off, because he has an artistic identity as a painter from the first. Weegee blazed out space for his Expressionism in a genre that, for all outward appearances, kept him a colorful hack. Klein, for his part, was an uncontainable aesthetic guerrilla who made use of corporate sponsors for purposes at the edge of their taste, testing the axiom that the more they funded the more he could provoke. The entry of both men into the fashion world (a few shots by Weegee and a longer stint by Klein) coincided with the moment when editors decided they liked the frisson of models seen in working-class milieux. Coming from such precincts themselves, the photographers could have had only a volatile response toward such a condescending program (the have-nots as backdrop). ...Like Weegee in his fun-house mood, ultraquick reflexes and unstanchable energy that spilled over into such modes as film, Klein differed in that he had no psychic base. No one acted the poseur with more conviction. We're entitled to ask what a figure with such equivocal resources contributed to the art of photography....

Frank, though, and Klein brought to the decade a feeling for its woes which, in retrospect, synthesizes it for us.... For those who remember the era, these *photographic evocations of it have the keenest resonance; for those who came later, The Americans and New York offer a wondrous guide.*

Max Kozloff, Artforum, May 1981

Codes and signs

If we accept the idea that the fundamental trait of a photographer is curiosity, because photography shows us the world in a way that we would not see it in reality, Klein's role becomes crucial. Not because he's more curious than other photographers, but because he's curious about something else. In an age in which photography continues to be taken at face value, in which people still believe 'it's true because it's in a photo and the photo is in a newspaper', Klein does not present himself as an interpreter of the world, discovering things in order to show them to us. As many have noted, since his earliest work, a major graphic role is played in many of Klein's images by letters, words and other forms of writing. The conclusion has often been drawn that Klein was simply photographing the world as it is, with its cars and its cables, its chaos and its anxieties. But it also makes Klein a reader rather than an observer. A reader of his environment; a reader of signs that may be social, political, aesthetic or material; a reader of his own images. Through this, we gain a better understanding of the way he takes pictures. Klein picks up his camera whenever he wants to, or as others might pick up a book. A maker of books, Klein also reads the book of his surroundings at his own pace. And as a reader of the visual world, he also becomes an archaeologist, a decoder of signs, ranging from the neon lights of New York to the ideograms of Tokyo or the badges of communist militants. Rather than speaking of the world, that old humanist myth that photography still perpetuates, Klein sets out to read it, and in the process writes a history of the clashing signs that we see everywhere, surrounding faces whose psychological meaning is ultimately less important than the way that they reveal a coded situation. The wide-angle lens that captures crowds and spaces, the flash that illuminates the details: these are part of this reading, and allow the rest fade into the background. It is because of this that Klein's imitators – and they are legion – remain imitators. They thought that the means were the end, and that Klein was merely

establishing a new way of taking pictures, rather than giving himself
a means of capturing his own reading of the world and in the process
avoiding the greatest risk of photography, that of reducing it to a
series of tricks and instructions.

Photography and painting

*If we compare many of the paintings of the 1950s with William Klein's book on
New York, we must bow to the evidence: the artist-photographer saw more clearly
and closer to reality than the most intuitive of American painters. He confronted
his own view of things head on, rather than wallowing in aestheticism. Klein quite
literally went out into the streets when painters were still stuck in their studios,
reluctant to paint from photographic models.*

*The anonymous crowd on Fifth Avenue, the parades and festivities for
Thanksgiving or St Patrick's Day, subway exits, the advertisements that would
haunt Warhol and Rosenquist, gangs of youths, the car showrooms and bars that
would fascinate the Photorealists, the omnipresent dollar sign, the movie-house
box offices that later inspired George Segal, the police and the Salvation Army,
wandering madmen, nightwatchmen, blind beggars, night clubs, the news-
stands that intrigued Fromanger, baseball played in the street and on patches
of wasteground, the banking districts deserted on Sundays, Times Square and
its 'language of the night', parking lots, the phone booths that inspired Richard
Lindner, car graveyards, the garbage dumps that were dredged for ideas by Arman
and César, the bridges over the East River, symbols of the conquering excess that
created all of these catastrophes that are as beautiful as they are ugly, and which,
since the late 1950s, have led to the complete overthrow of the contemporary
language of aesthetics: these are the subjects that William Klein was the first to
tackle with lucidity and power. The entire catalogue of new subjects for painting
can be seen there, several years in advance, and without anyone seeming to have
ever noticed it. It is a world worth dreaming about.*

Alain Jouffroy, Zoom, 1973

Strange tales

The happily unclassifiable Klein, the American in Paris, not truly
accepted on the far side of the Atlantic but not quite in tune with
the aesthetics of his homeland, the man who never built a career as
a photographer because he had better things to do, the Klein who

has spent thirty years speed-reading the streets and their images: this Klein invented a new form of the method of permanently recording the world that we call photography. Although it bears the hallmarks of his personality, for cultural reasons his style seems to belong to the theatre of the absurd, not in the French sense of the term but in a special New York Jewish sense, full of black comedy and anxious laughter. Klein's recognition by the wider world of photography – such as his inclusion in this series of books, for instance – could also be seen as part of this logic of the absurd. Since Klein has never been one for groups or movements, it could surely be said that he now occupies a rather strange place in the story of photography. But what a story, in any case. What a strange story.

Christian Caujolle

1. Gun 1, Amsterdam Avenue, New York, 1954.

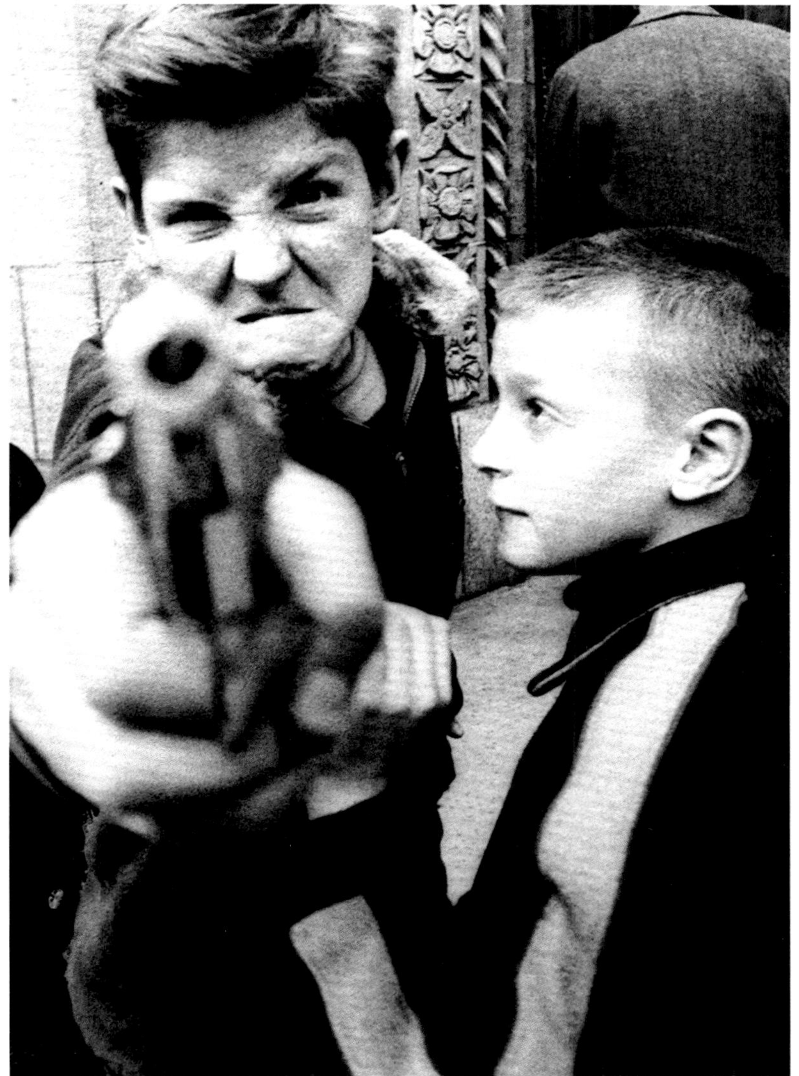

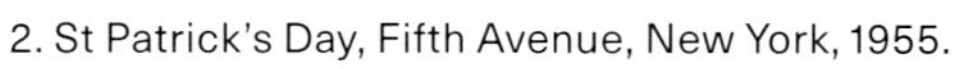

2. St Patrick's Day, Fifth Avenue, New York, 1955.

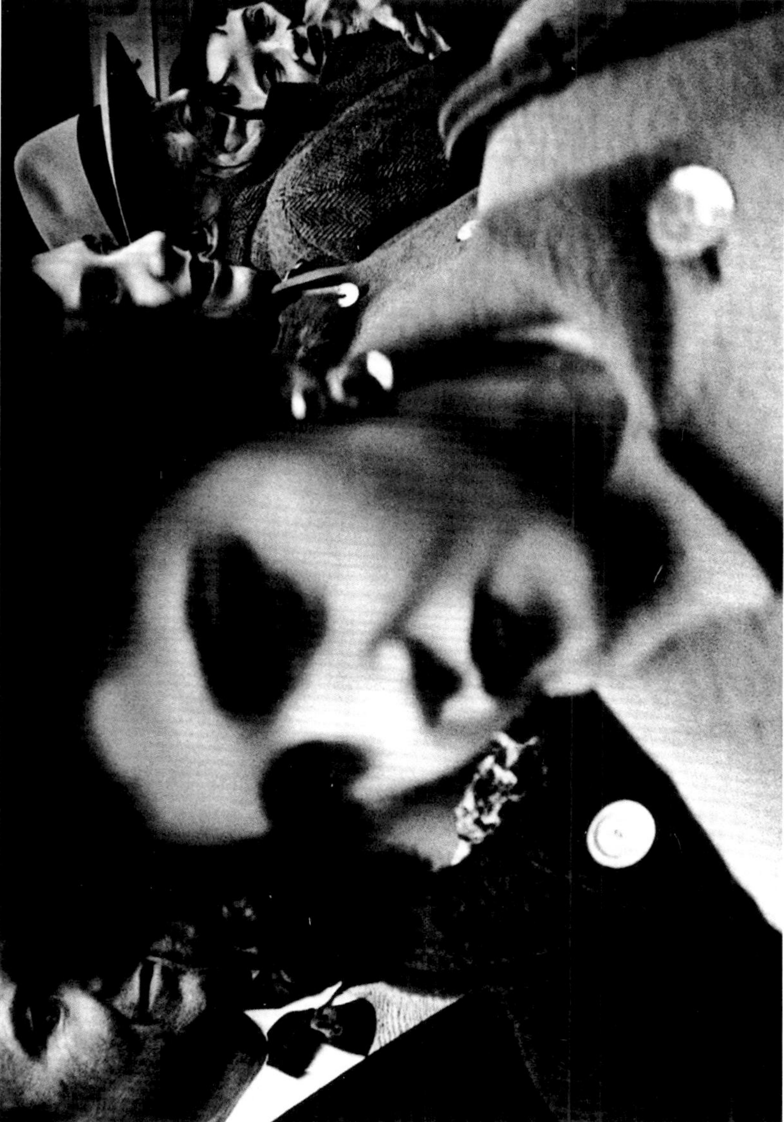

3. Gun 2, Little Italy, New York, 1954.

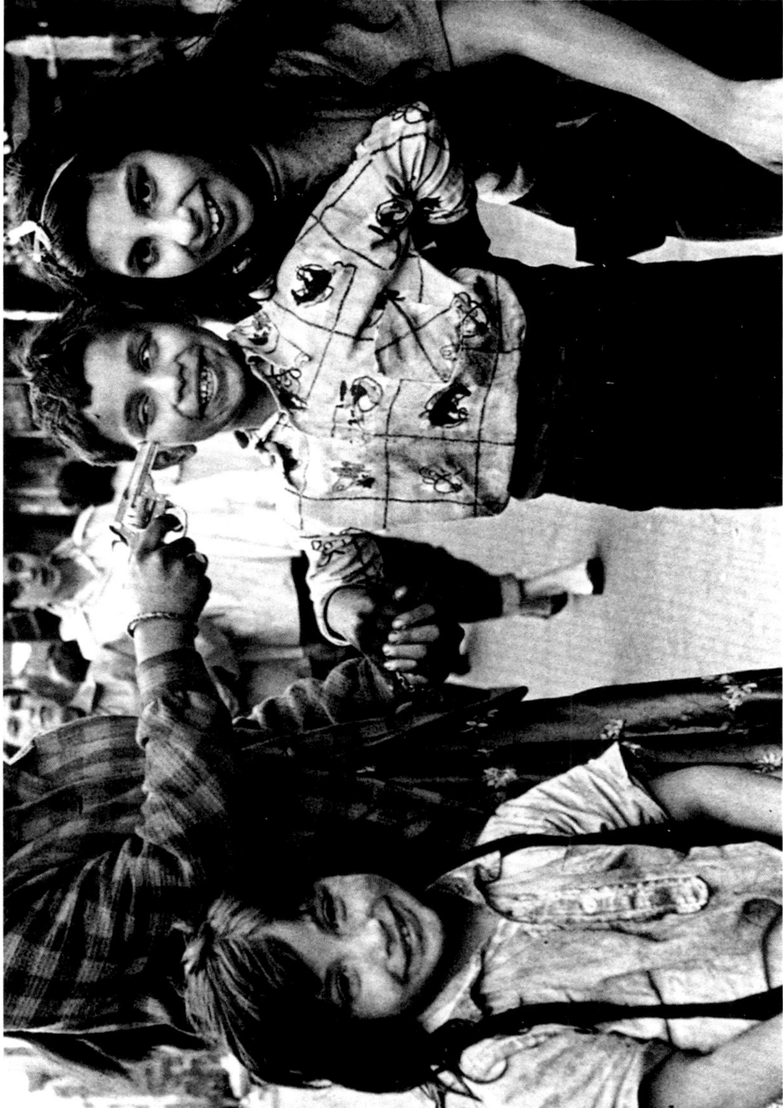

4. New York, 1954.

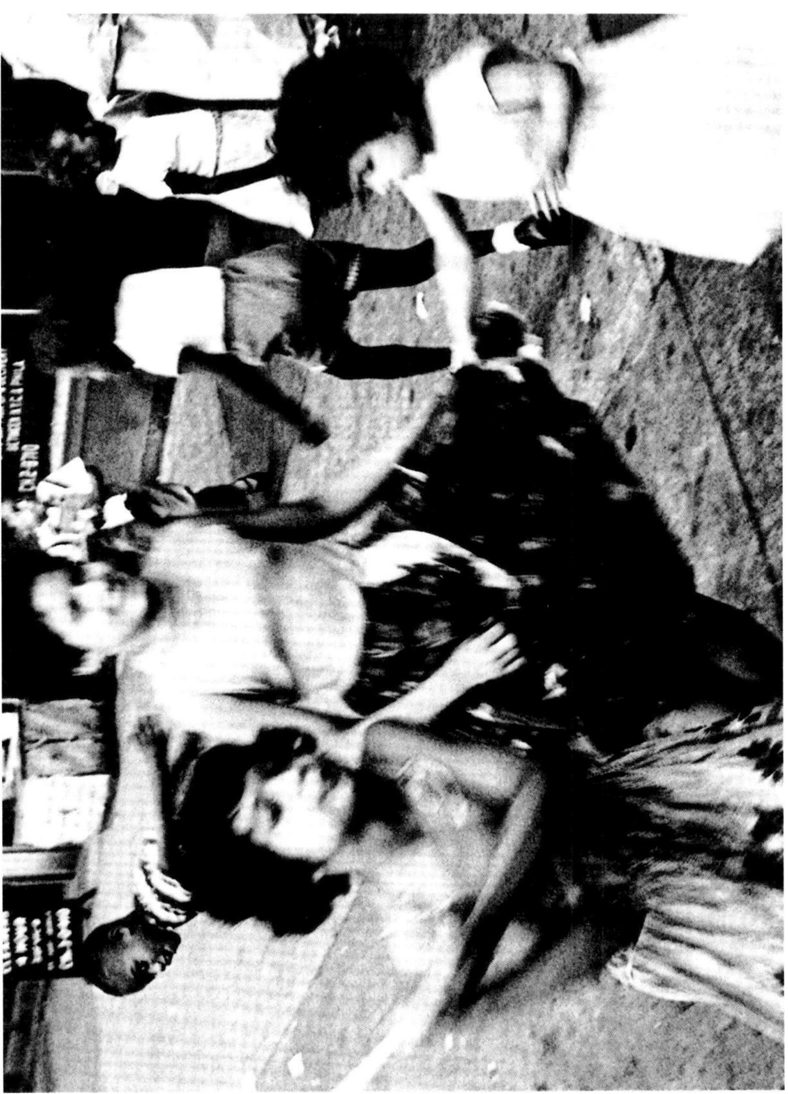

5. Dance in Brooklyn, New York, 1955.

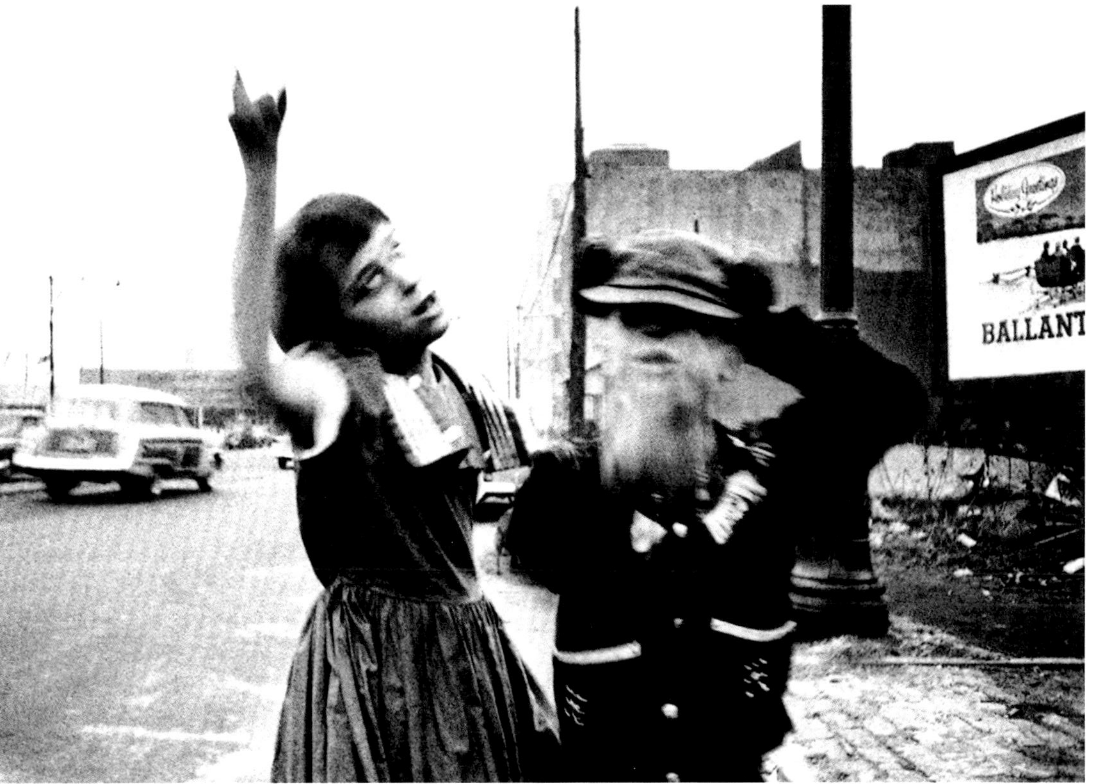
BALLANTINE

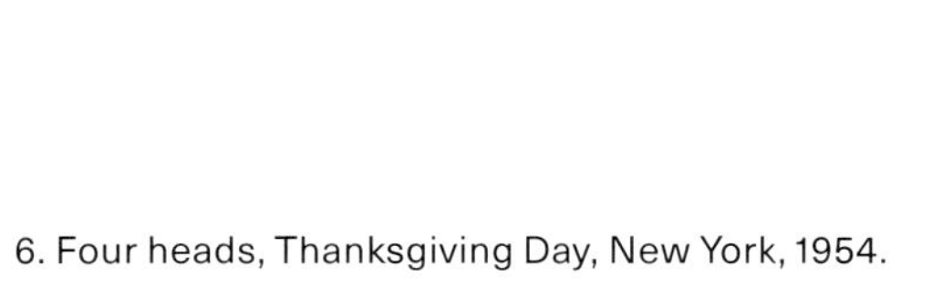

6. Four heads, Thanksgiving Day, New York, 1954.

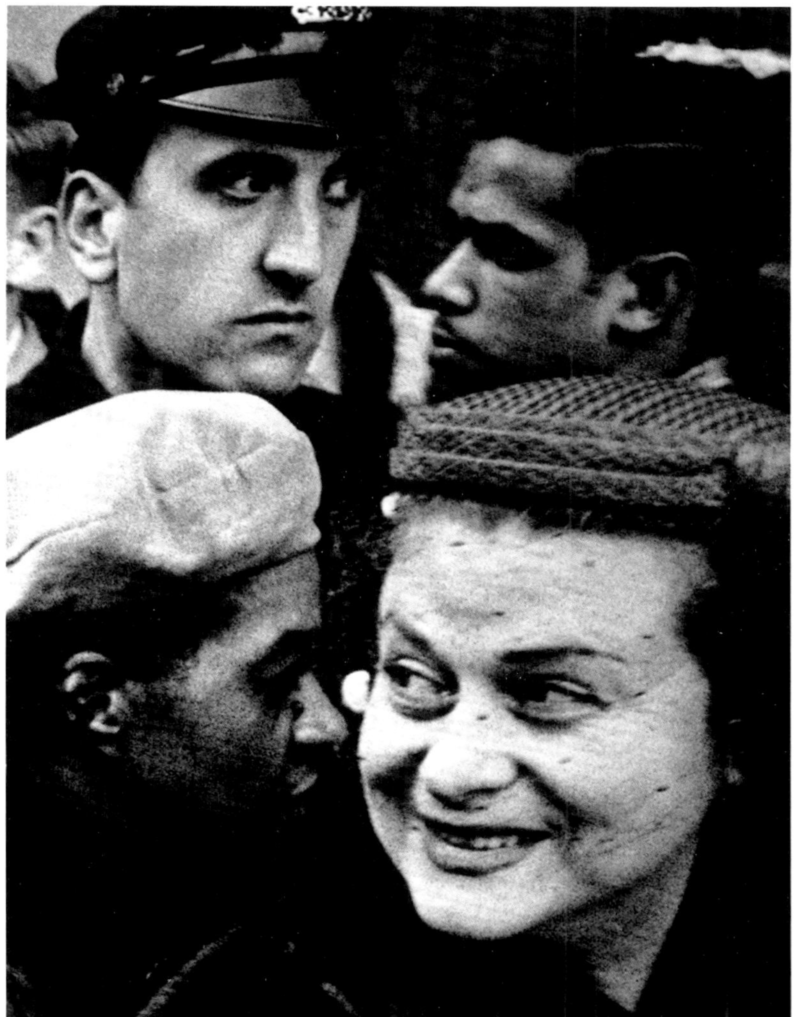

7. St Patrick's Day, New York, 1955.

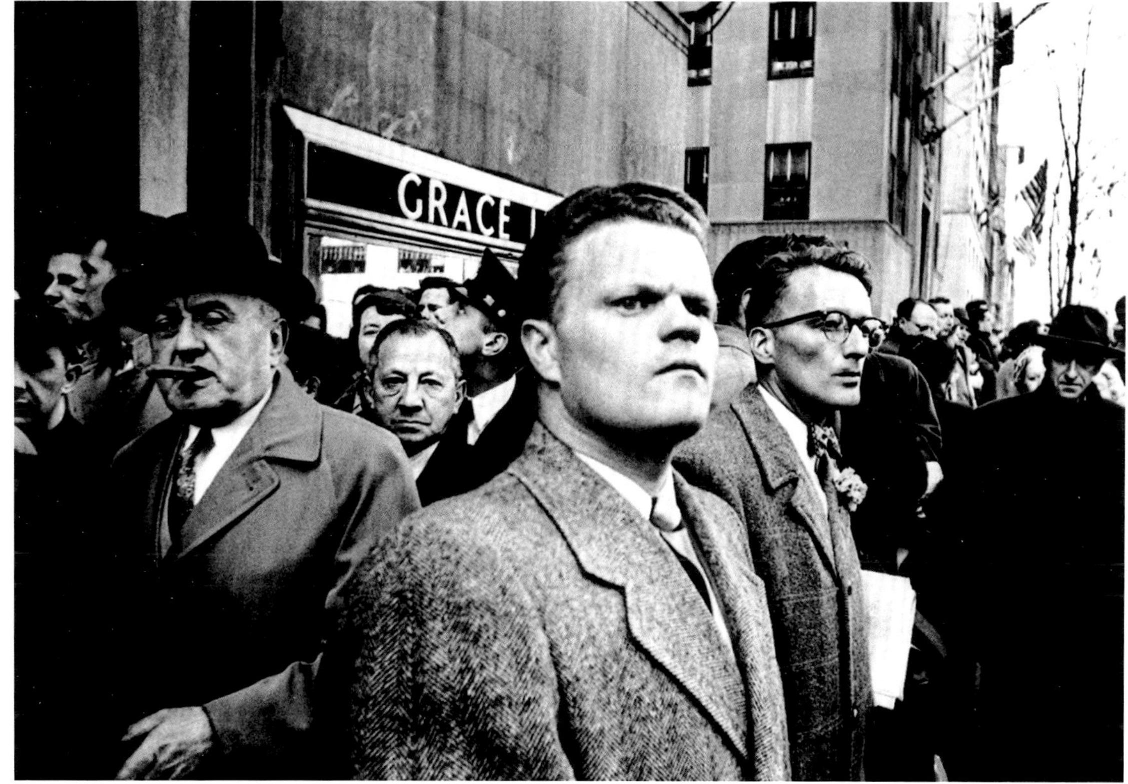
GRACE

8. Outside Macy's, New York, 1955.

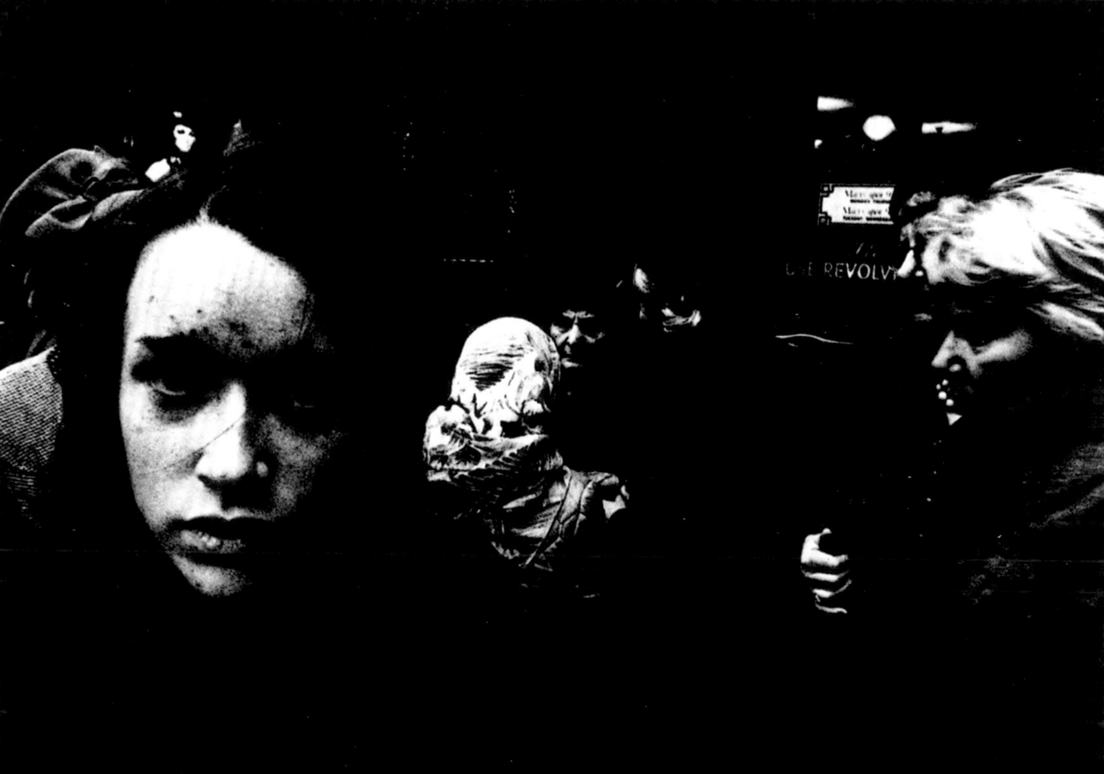
THE REVOLV

9. Candy store, New York, 1955.

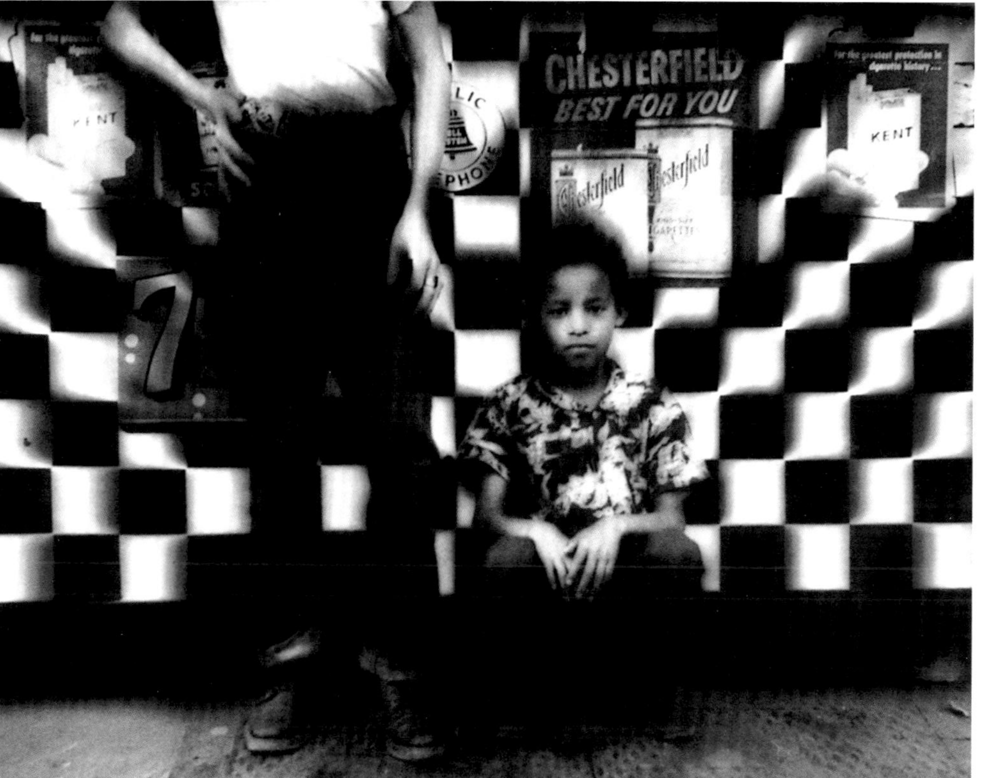

KENT
for the greatest protection in cigarette history...
CHESTERFIELD
BEST FOR YOU
Chesterfield
Chesterfield
KING-SIZE CIGARETTES
PUBLIC
BELL SYSTEM
TELEPHONE
KENT
for the greatest protection in cigarette history...

10. Charity ball, Waldorf, New York, 1955.

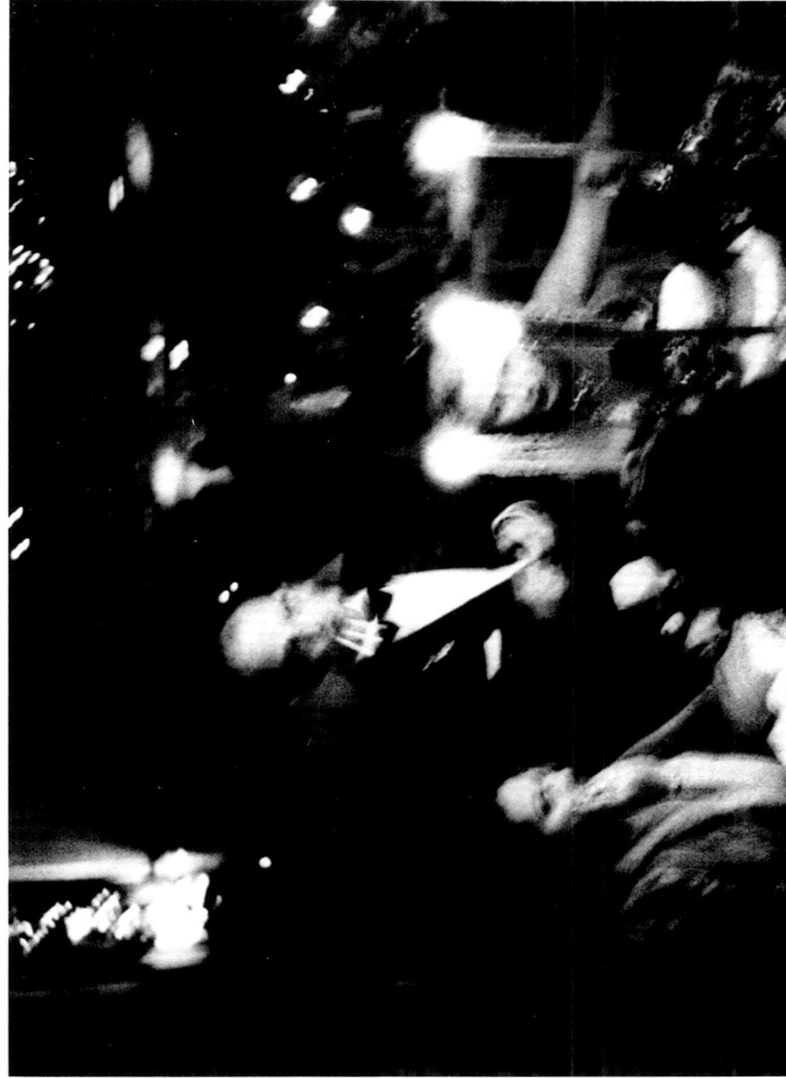

11. Winter, Coney Island, New York, 1955.

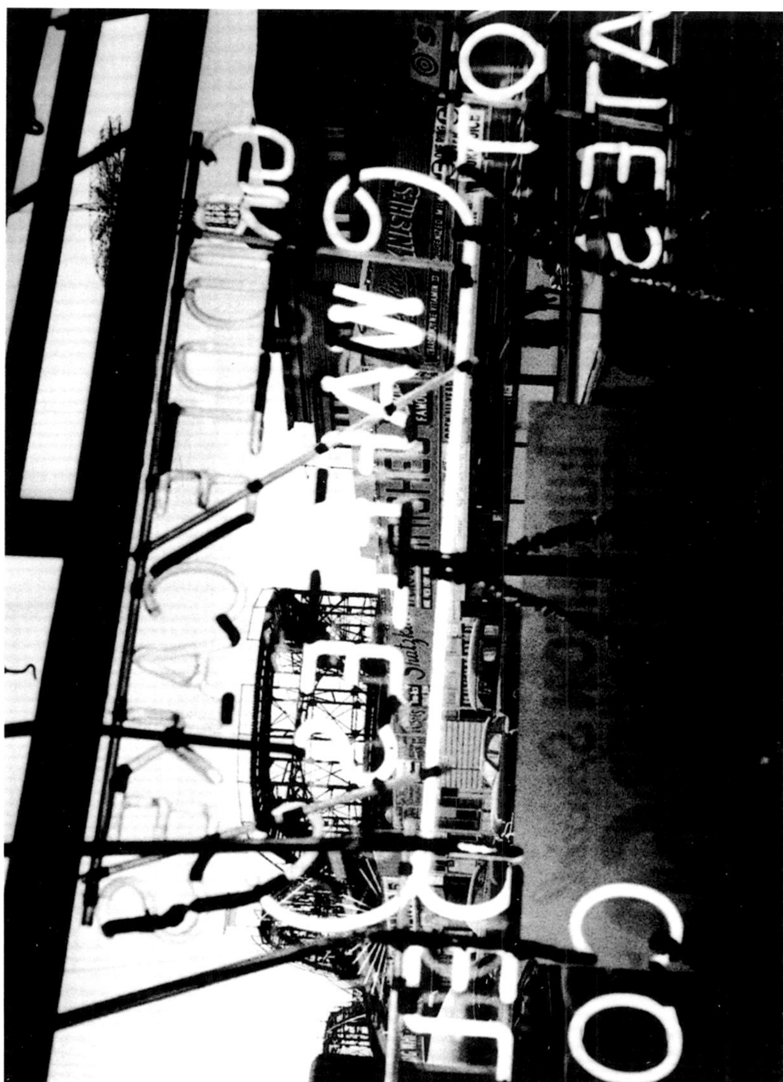

12. Watching a parade, New York, 1955.

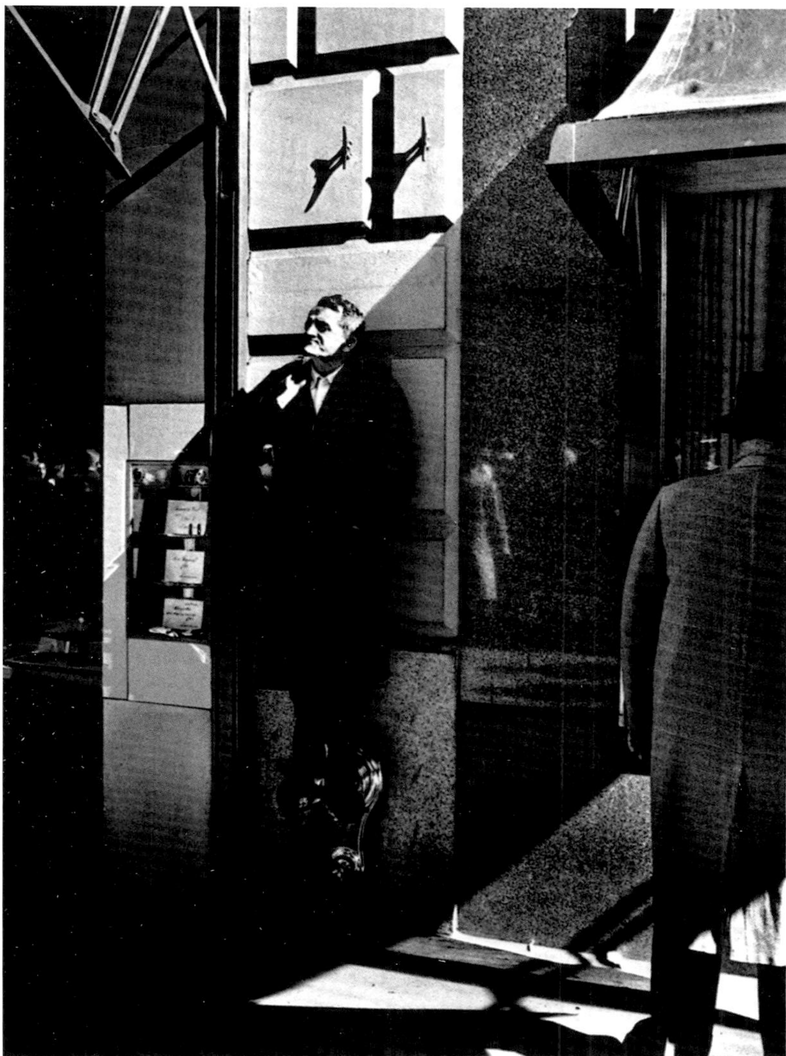

13. 75 + Fight Communism, New York, 1955.

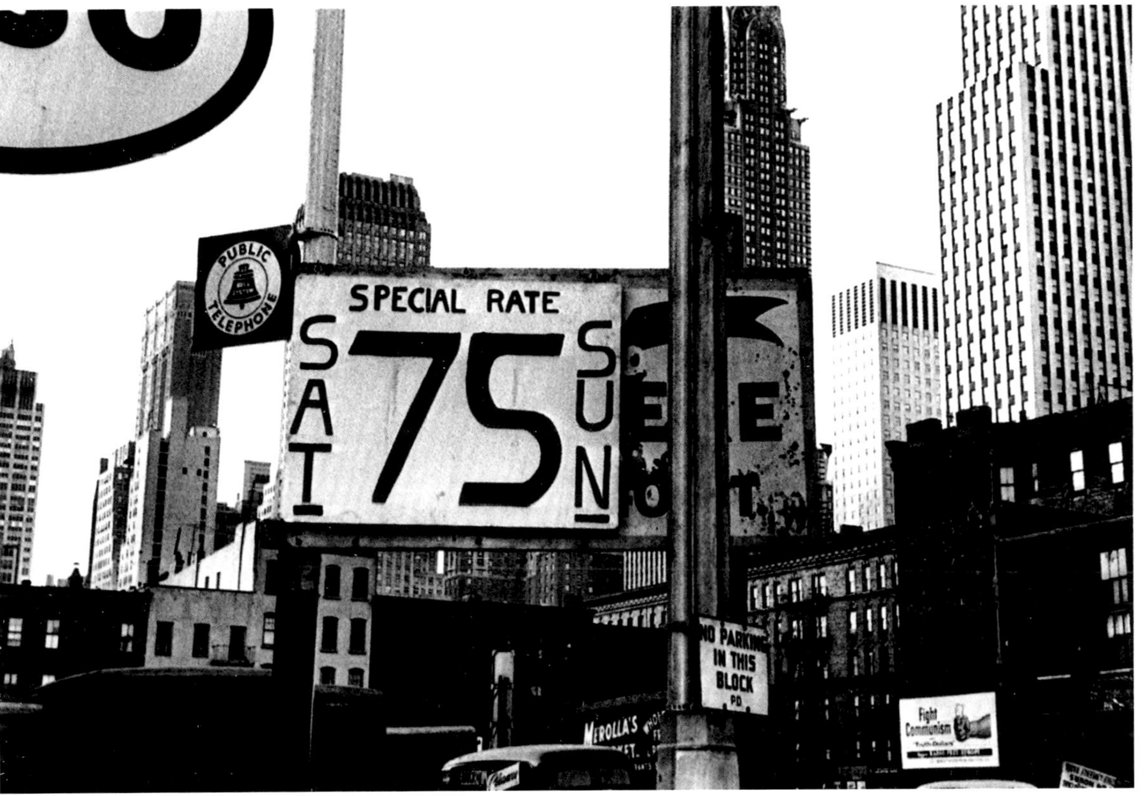
PUBLIC TELEPHONE
SPECIAL RATE
SAT 75 SUN
NO PARKING IN THIS BLOCK
PD
MEROLLA'S
Fight Communism

14. Pigeons, unchained, Broadway, New York, 1955.

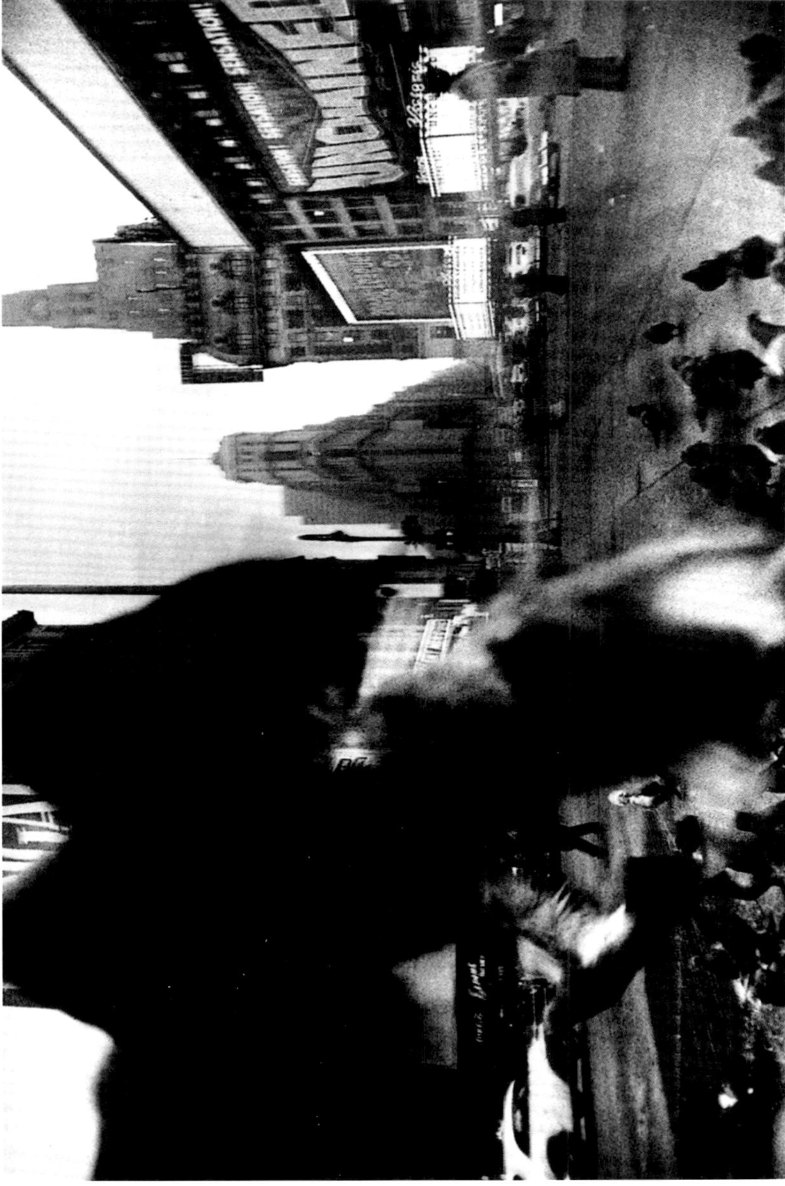

15. Elvis, New York, 1963.

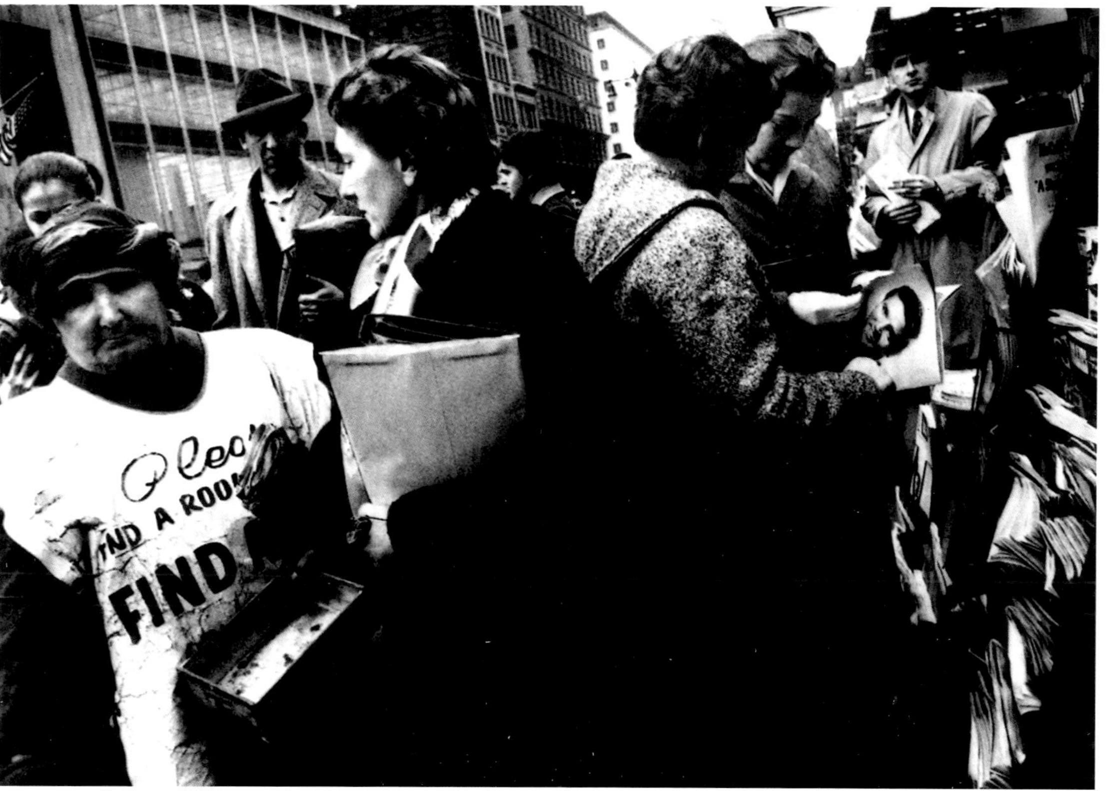
Plea
ND A ROOM
FIND

16. Corner cigar store, New York, 1983.

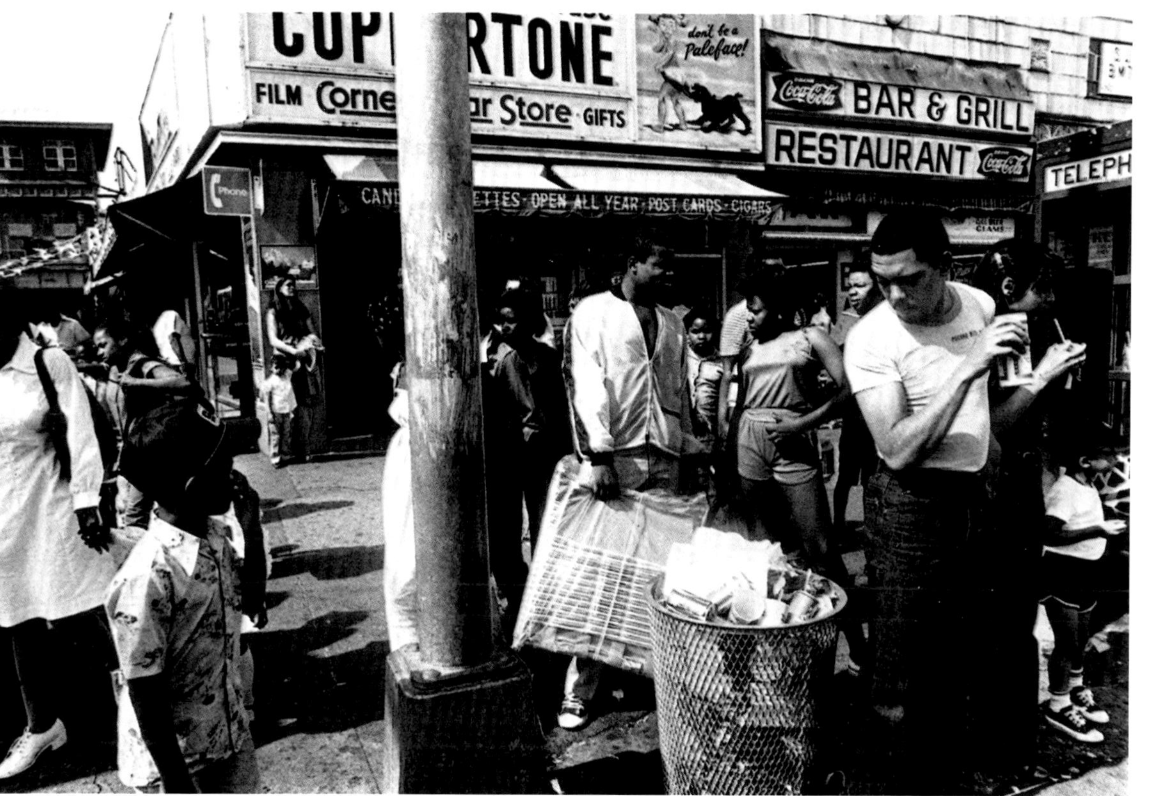
COPPERTONE
don't be a Paleface!
FILM Corner Store · GIFTS
Coca-Cola BAR & GRILL
RESTAURANT Coca-Cola
TELEPH
Phone
CAND ETTES · OPEN ALL YEAR · POST CARDS · CIGARS

17. Colosseo Quadrato + Buitoni, Rome, 1956.

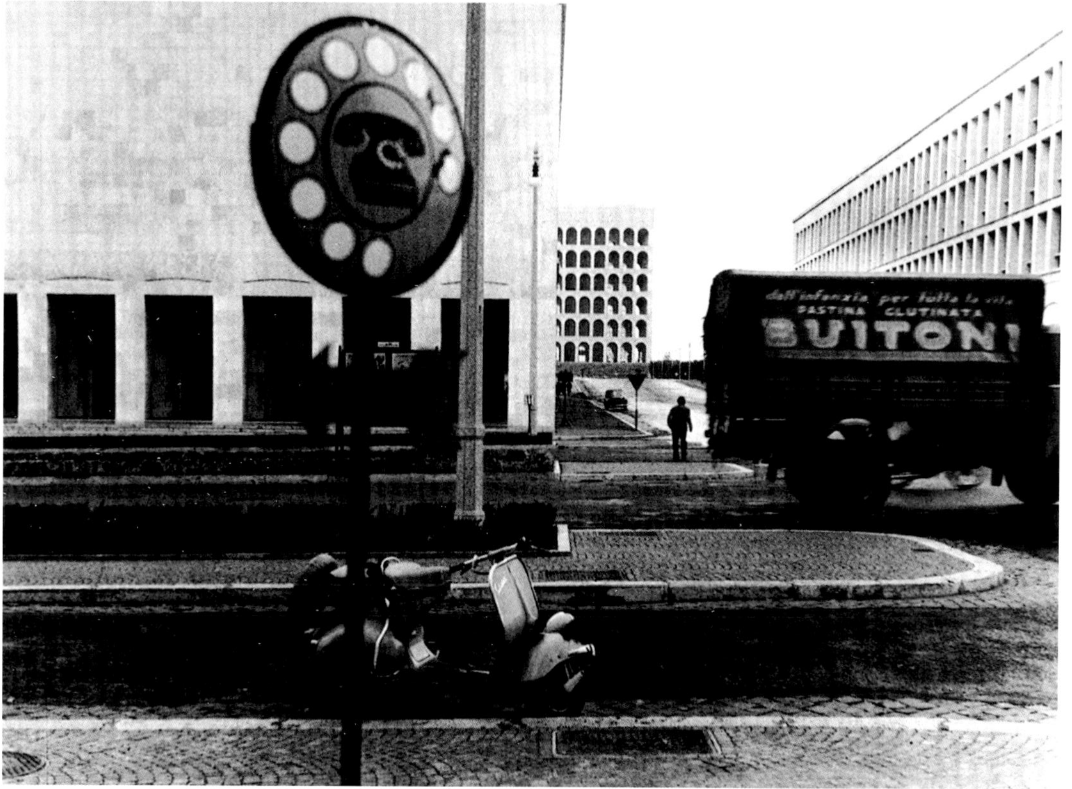
dall'infanzia per tutta la vita
PASTINA GLUTINATA
BUITONI

18. Tramway, Madrid, 1956.

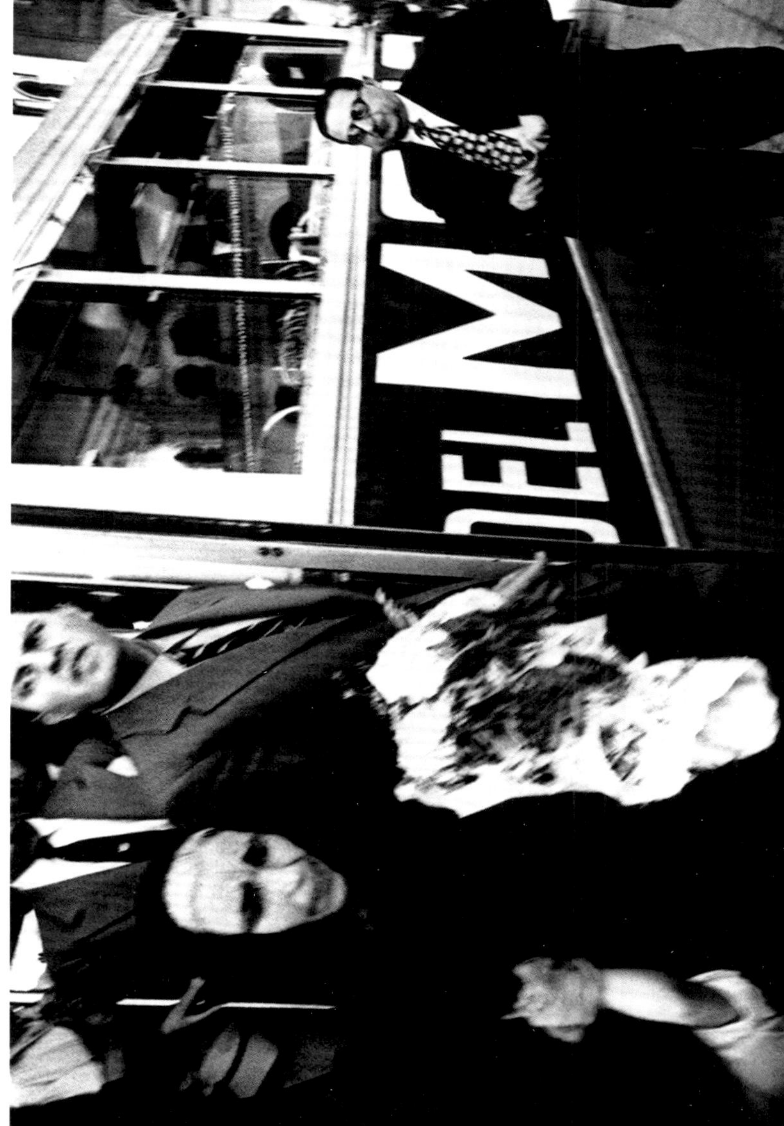

19. Hand, Beirut, 1963.

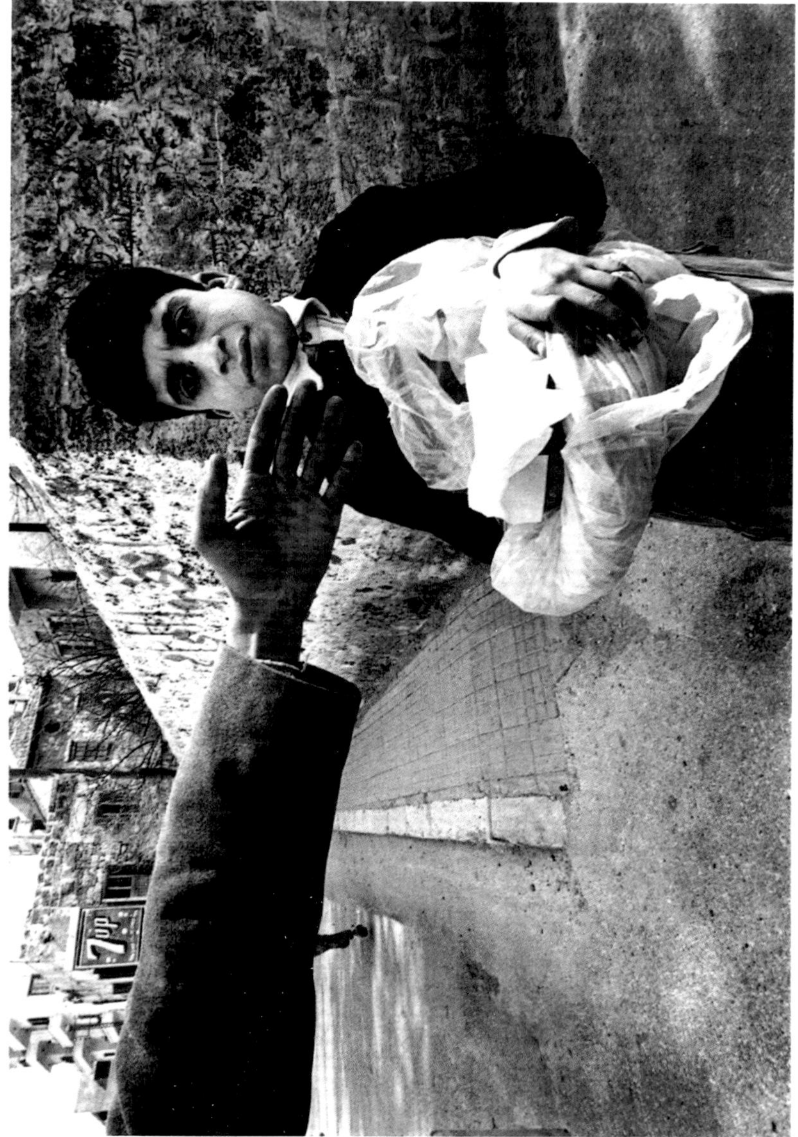

20. Watchman, Cinecittà, Rome, 1956.

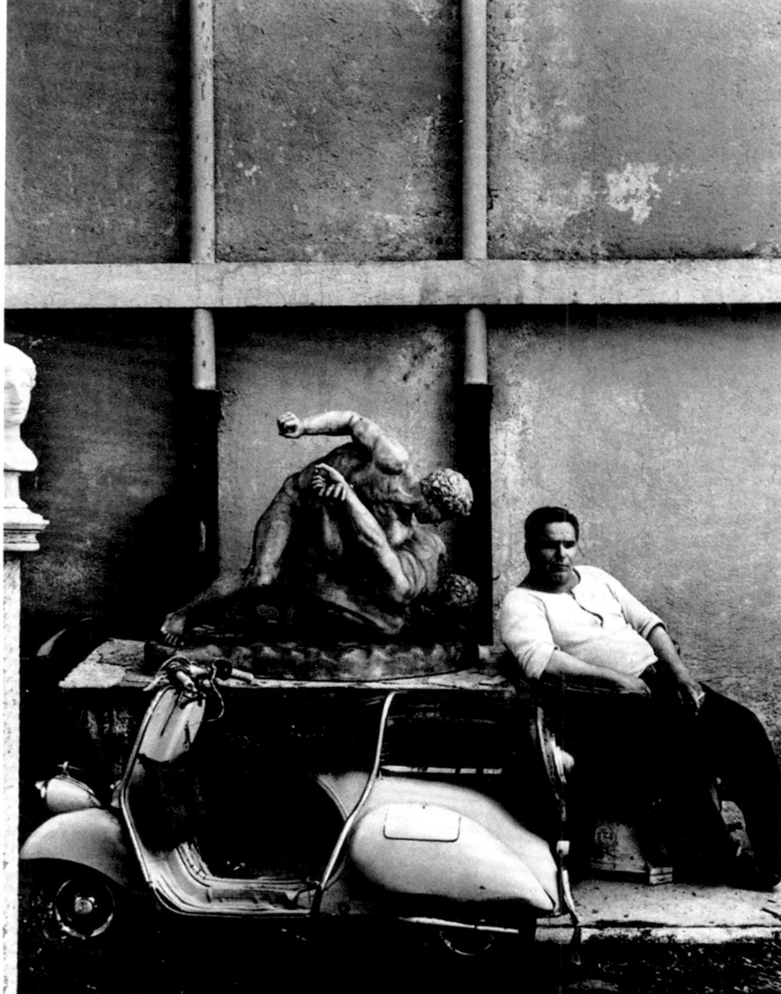

21. Ostia Beach, Rome, 1956.

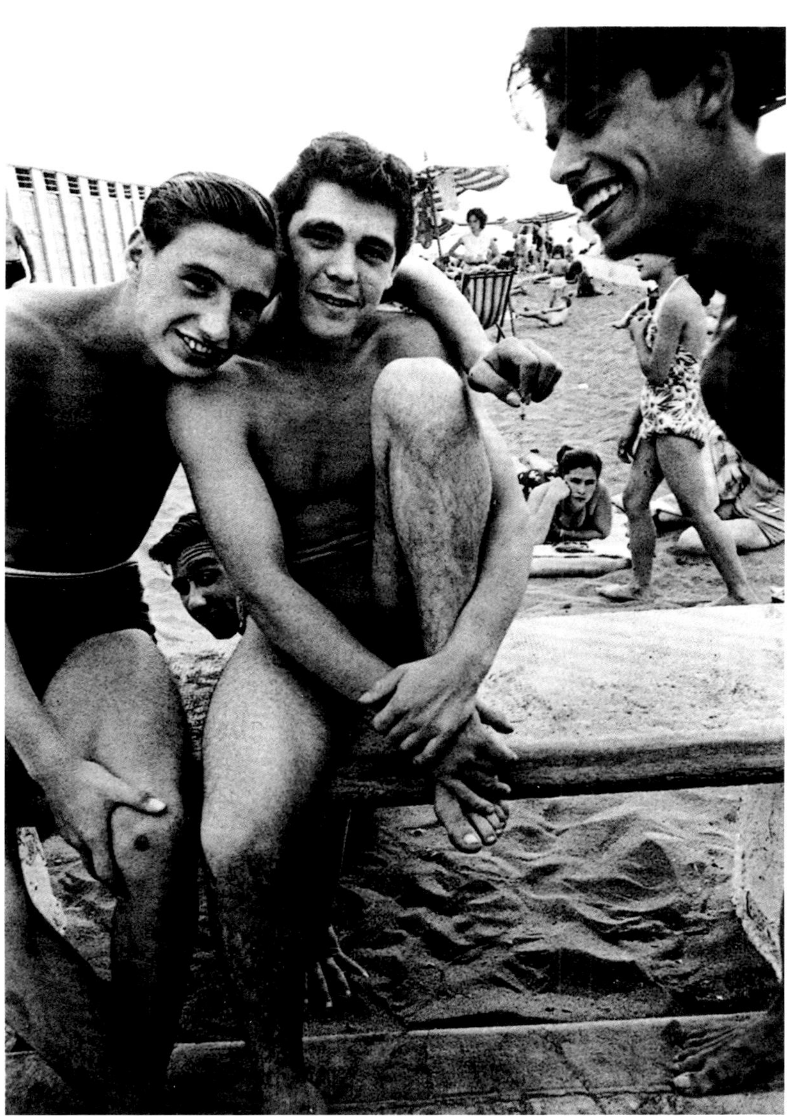

22. Red light, Via Flaminia, Rome, 1956.

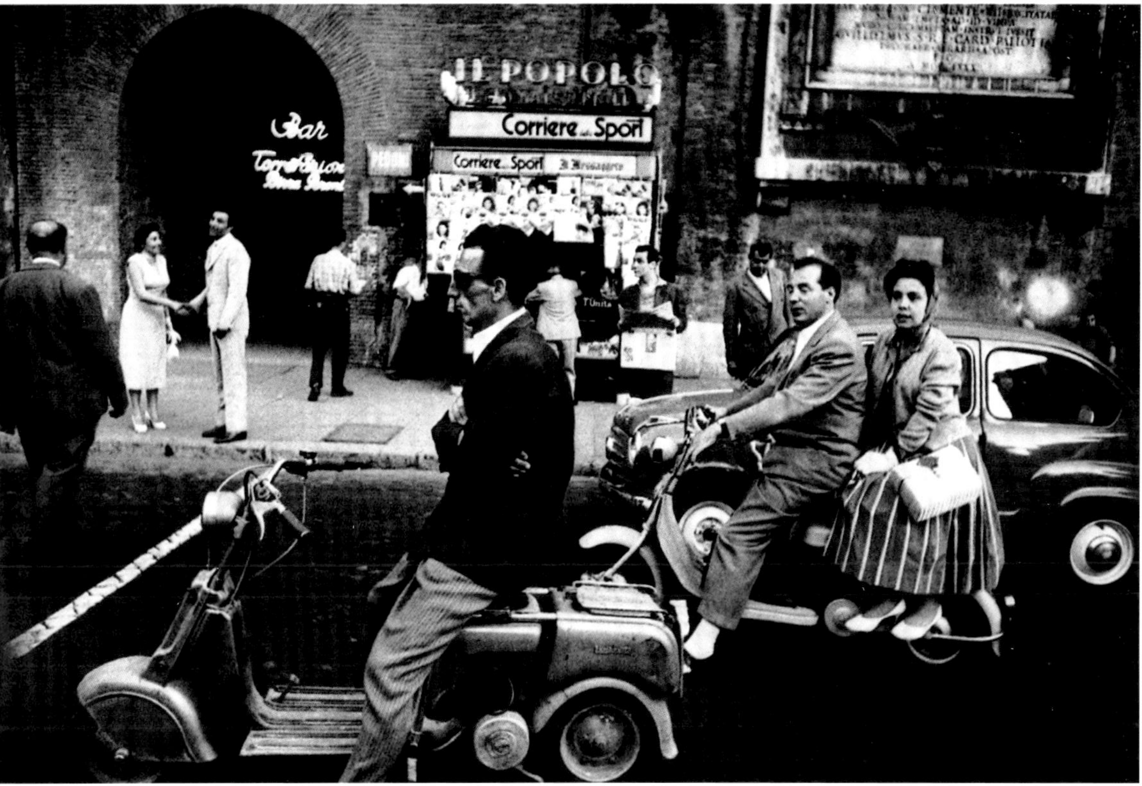
Bar
IL POPOLO
Corriere dello Sport
Corriere dello Sport
l'Unità

23. Barber shop, Rome, 1956

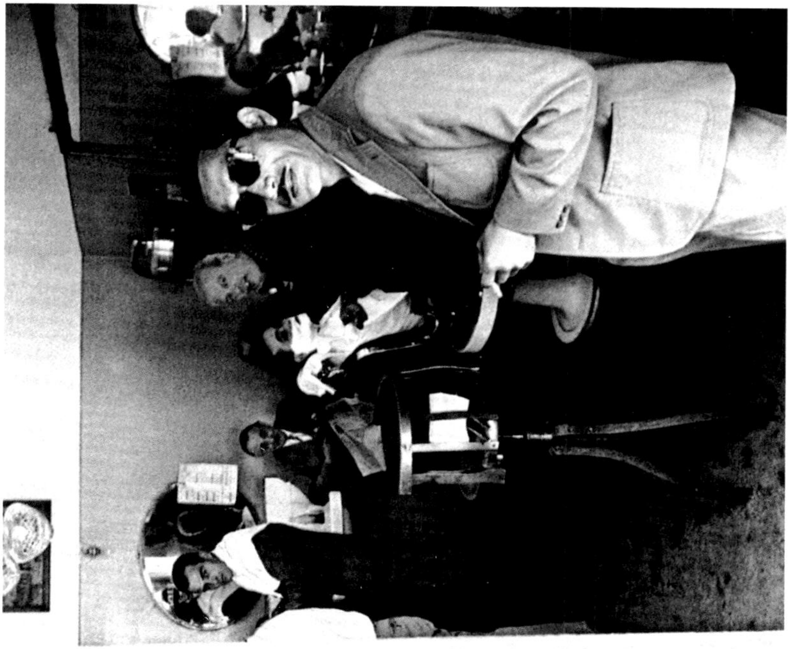

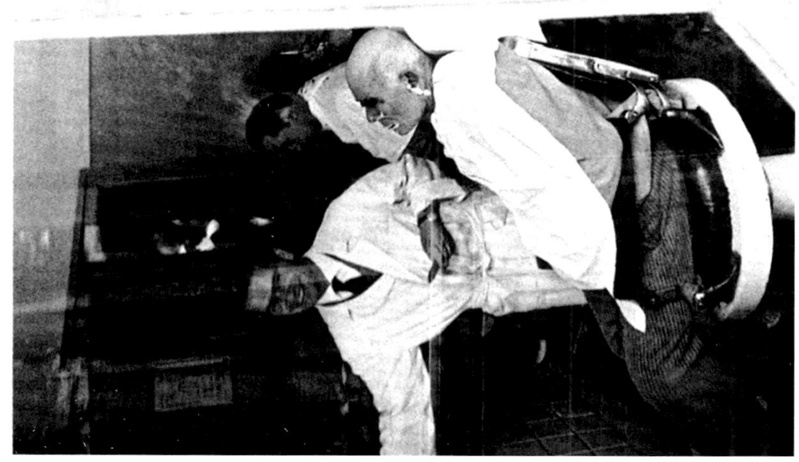

24. Aleksandra Yablochkina, the Sarah
Bernhardt of Russia, Moscow, 1960.

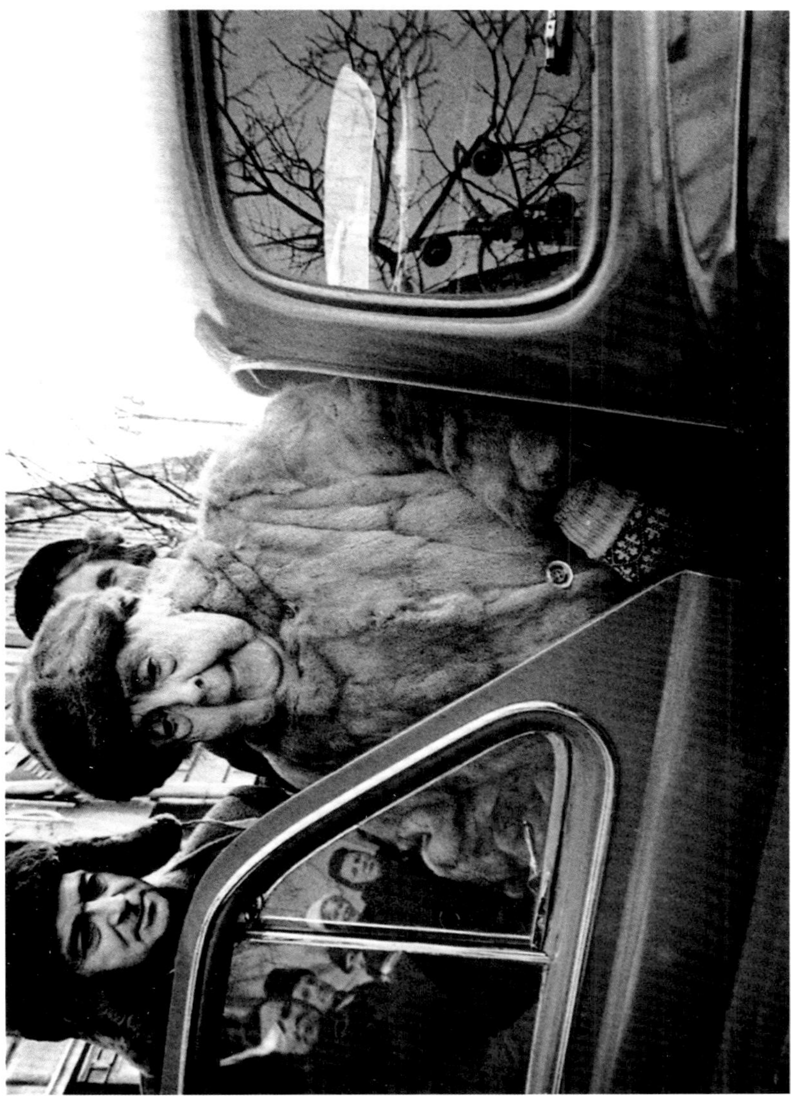

25. GUM department store, Moscow, 1960.

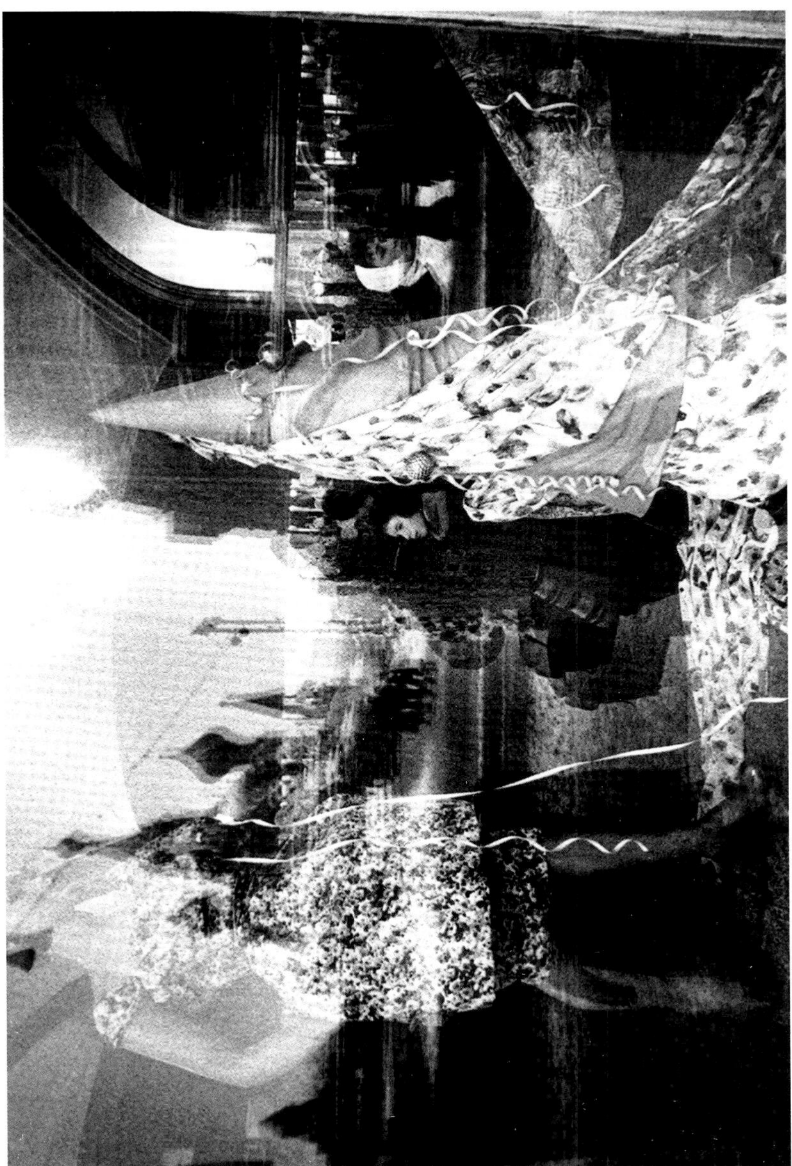

26. May Day parade, Moscow, 1961.

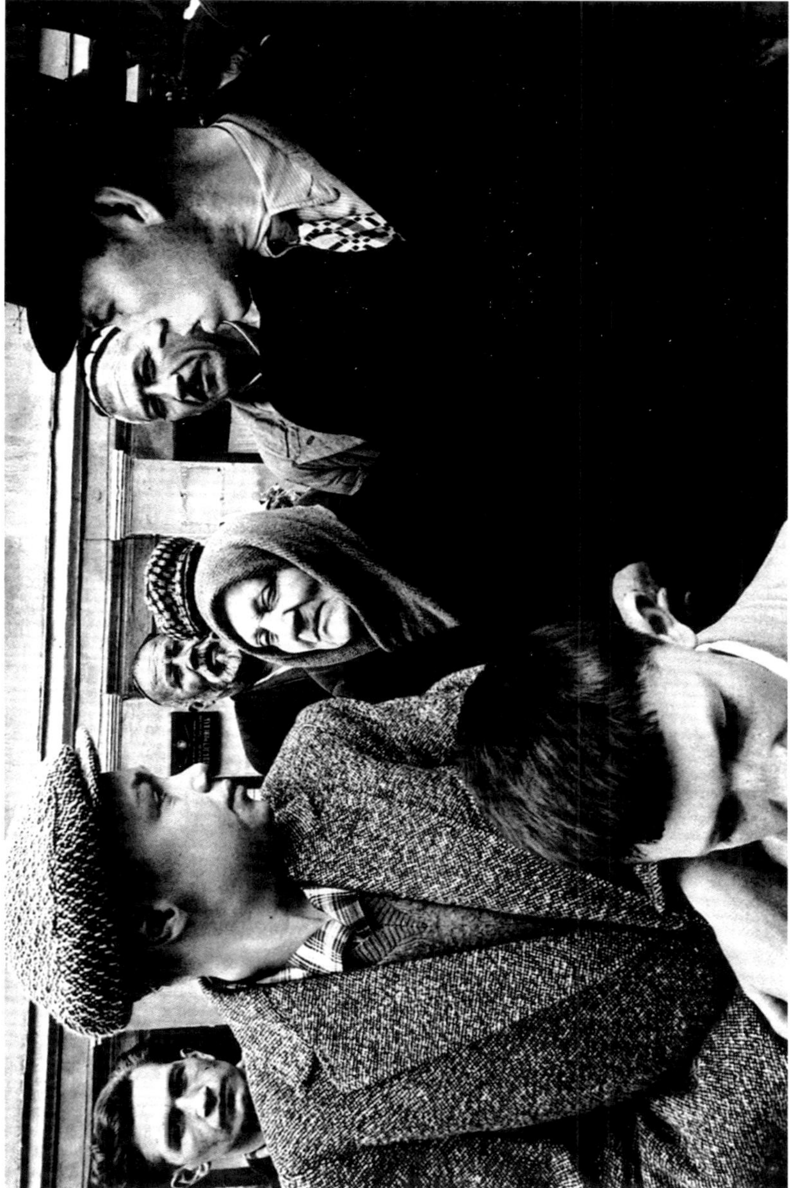

27. Gorky Park, Moscow, 1959.

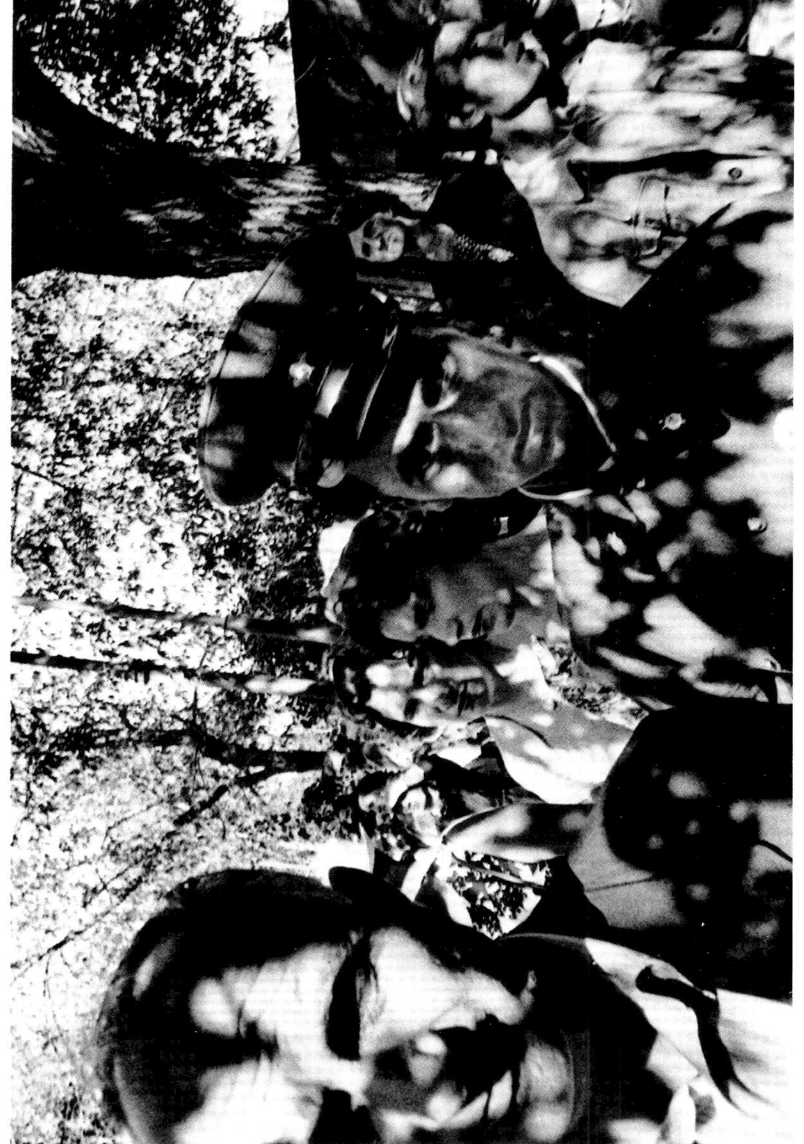

28. Bikini, Moscow, 1959.

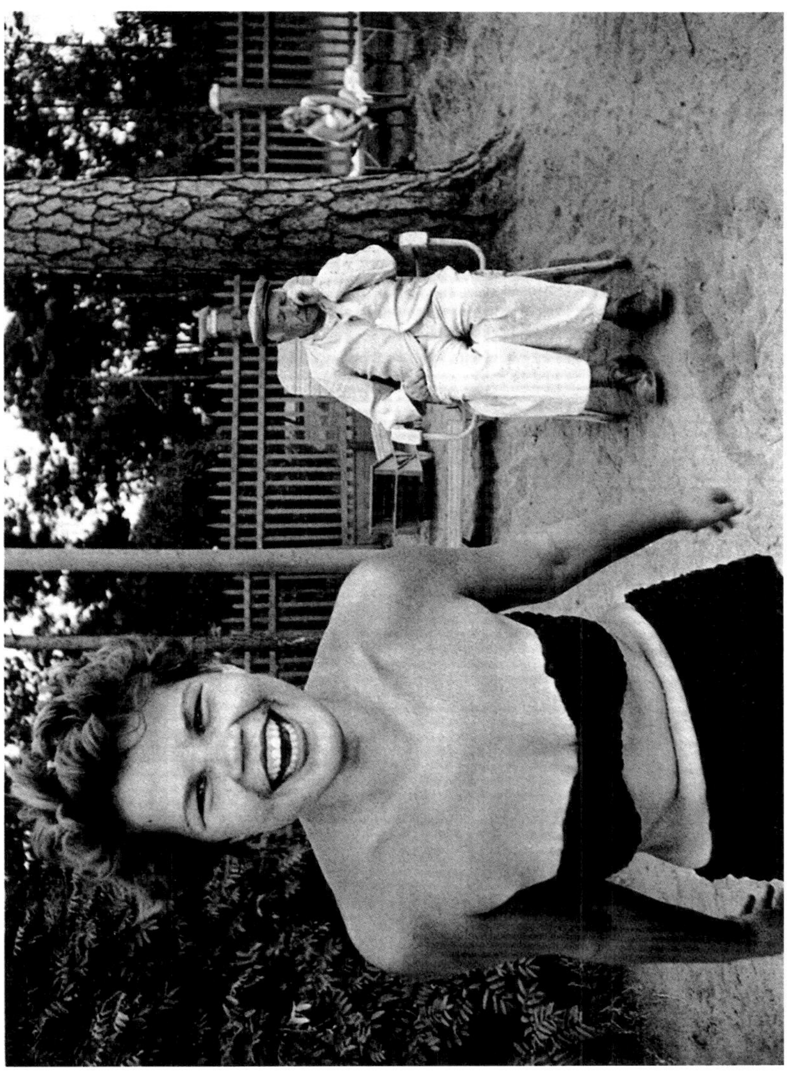

29. Table tennis, Moscow, 1959.

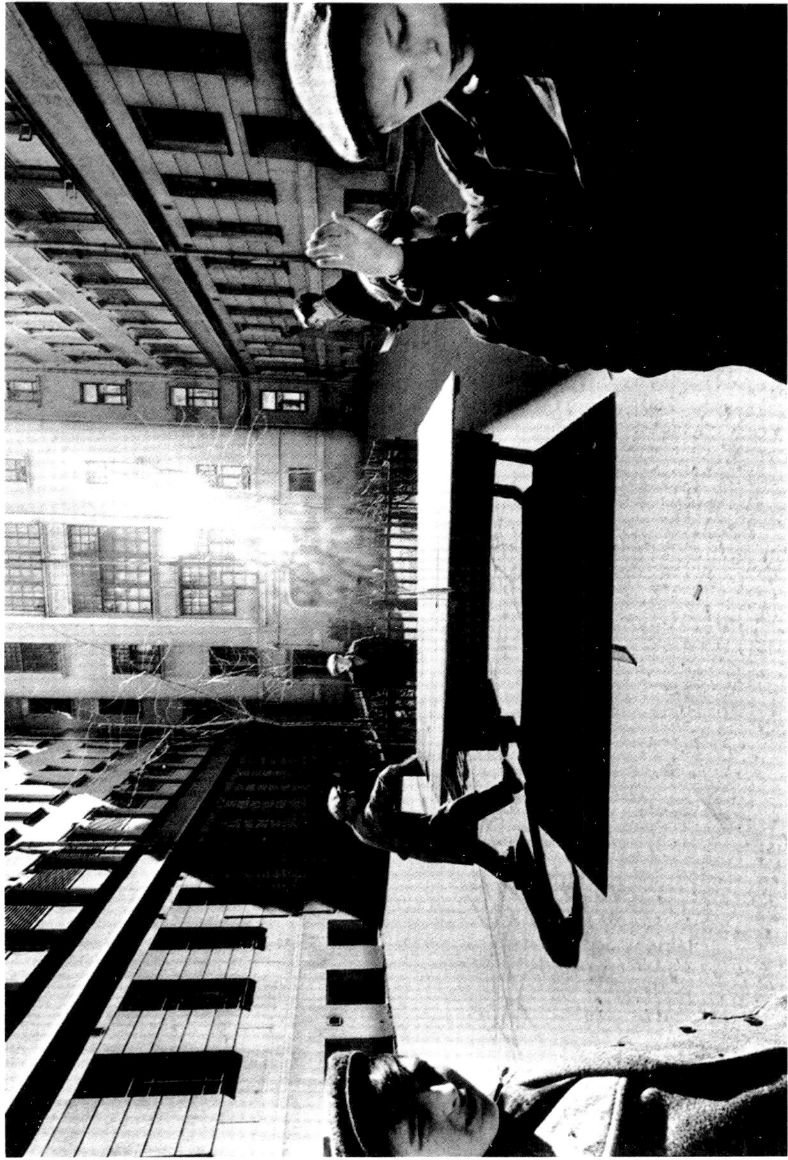

30. Kiev Station, Moscow, 1959.

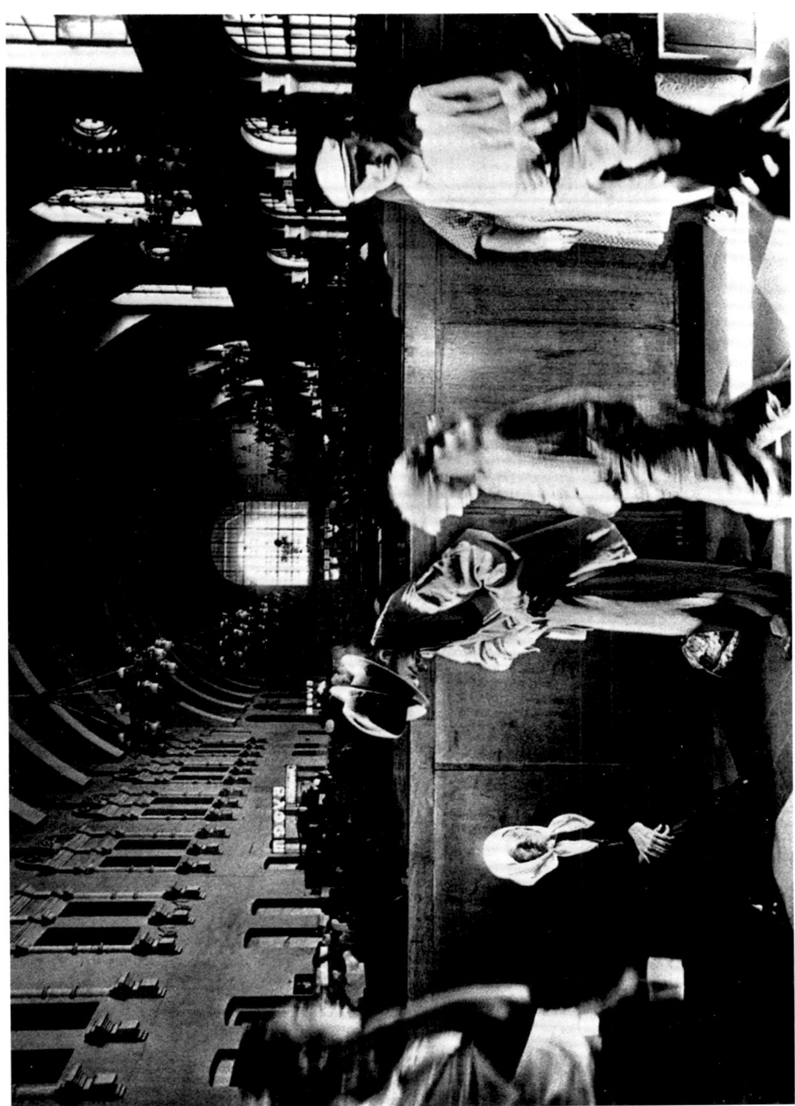

31. Actors' Union Praesidium, Moscow, 1960.

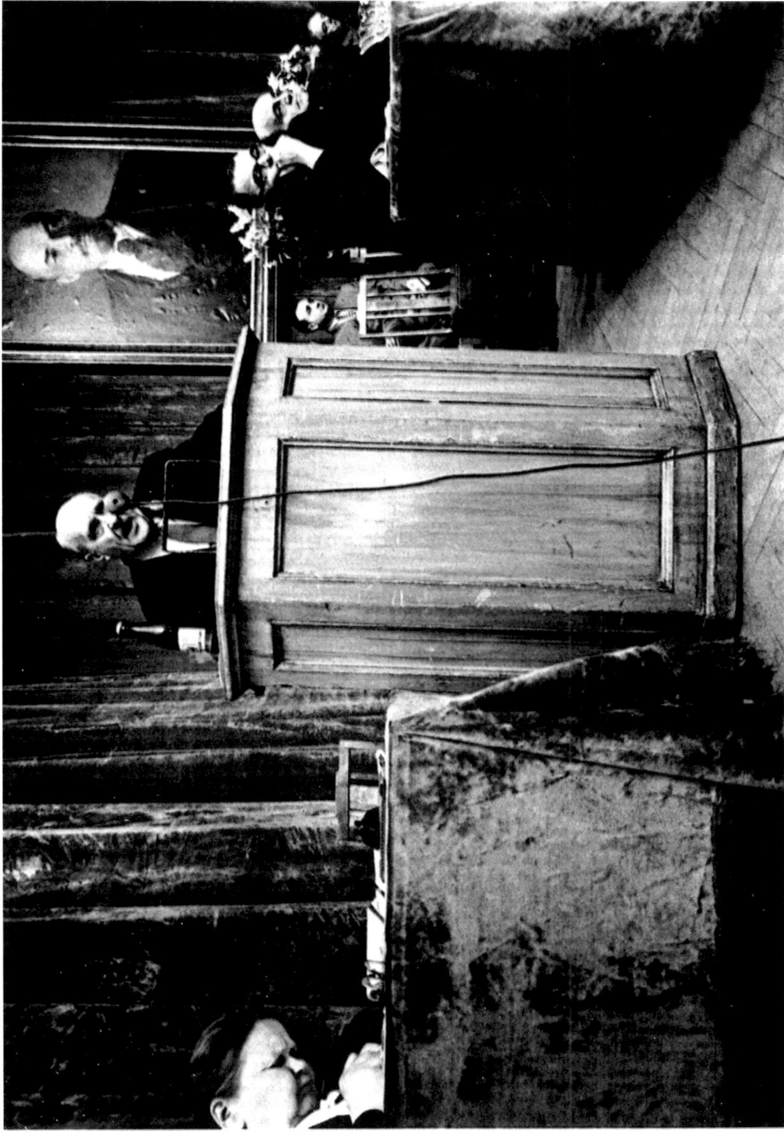

32. Cinema poster, Tokyo, 1961.

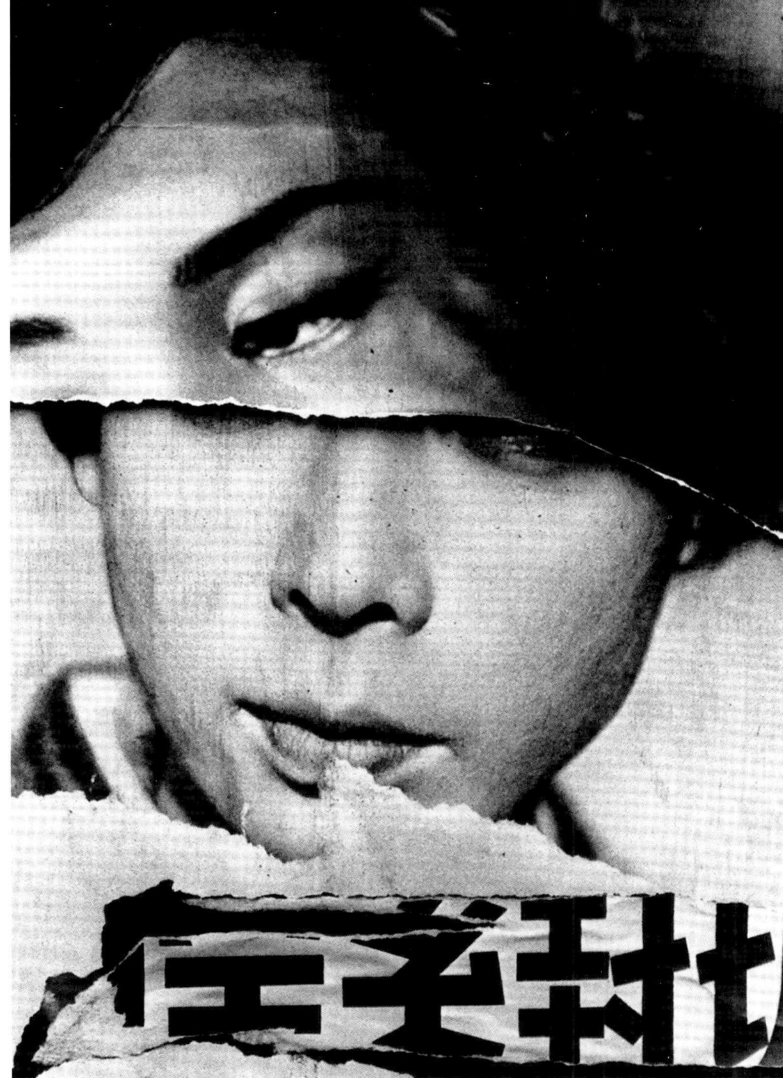

33. Shinohara, fighter-painter, Tokyo, 1961.

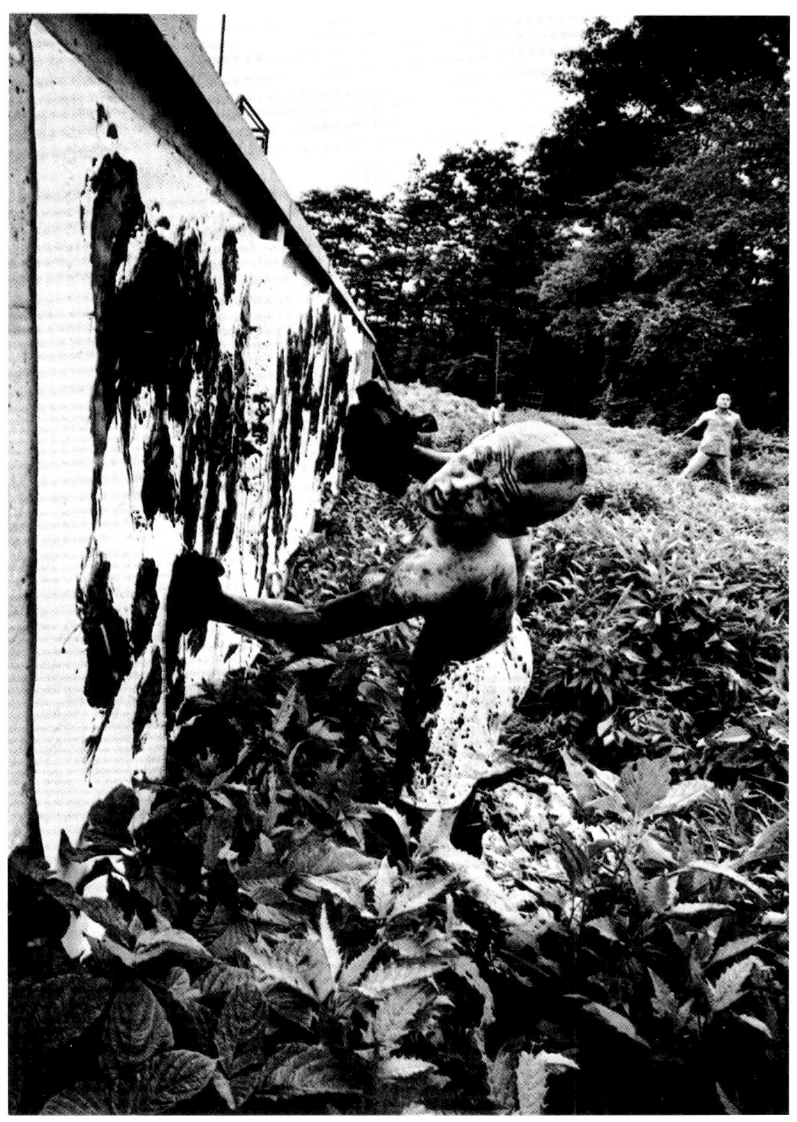

34. Dance happening, Tokyo, 1961.

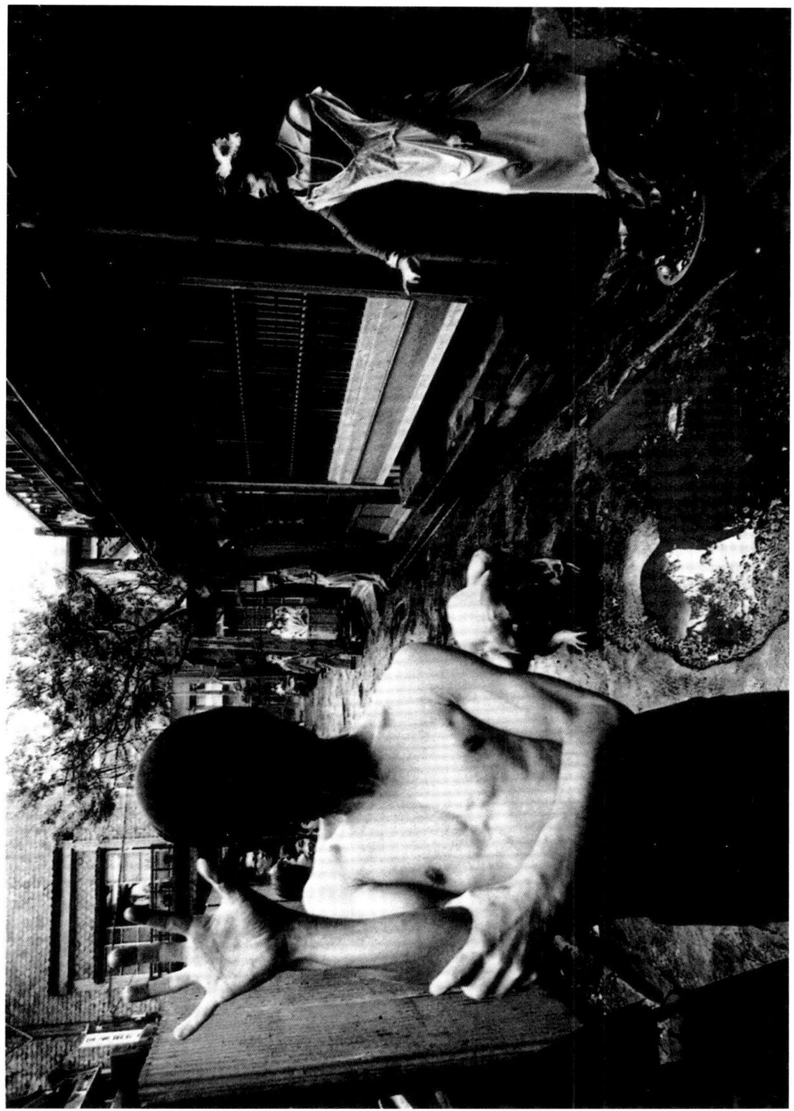

35. Bodybuilder, Tokyo, 1961.

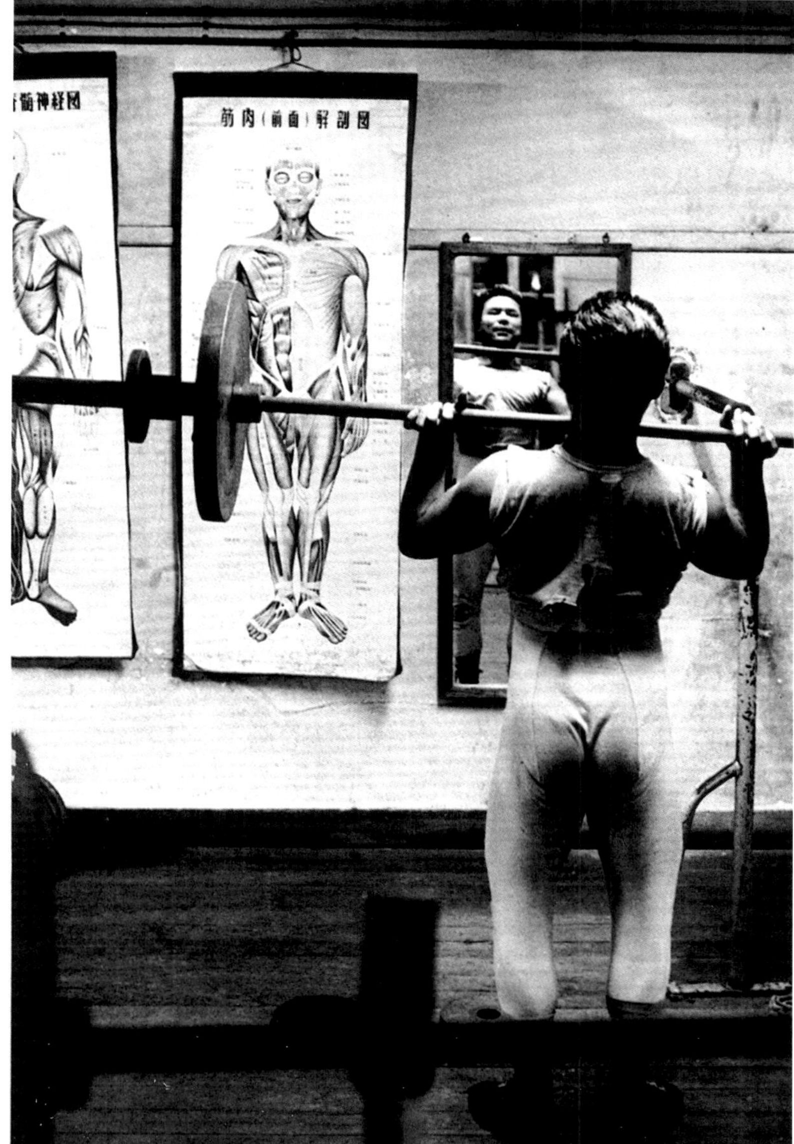
筋肉（前面）解剖図

36. Pachinko doorman, Tokyo, 1961.

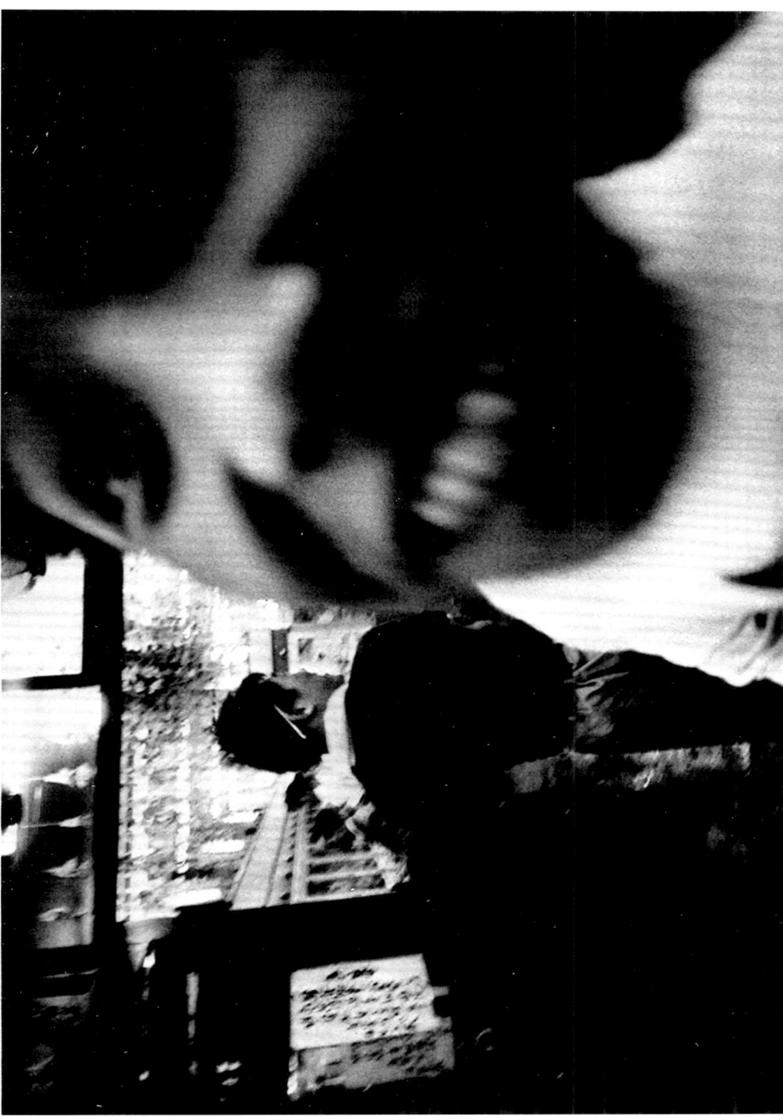

37. Apollo service station, Tokyo, 1961.

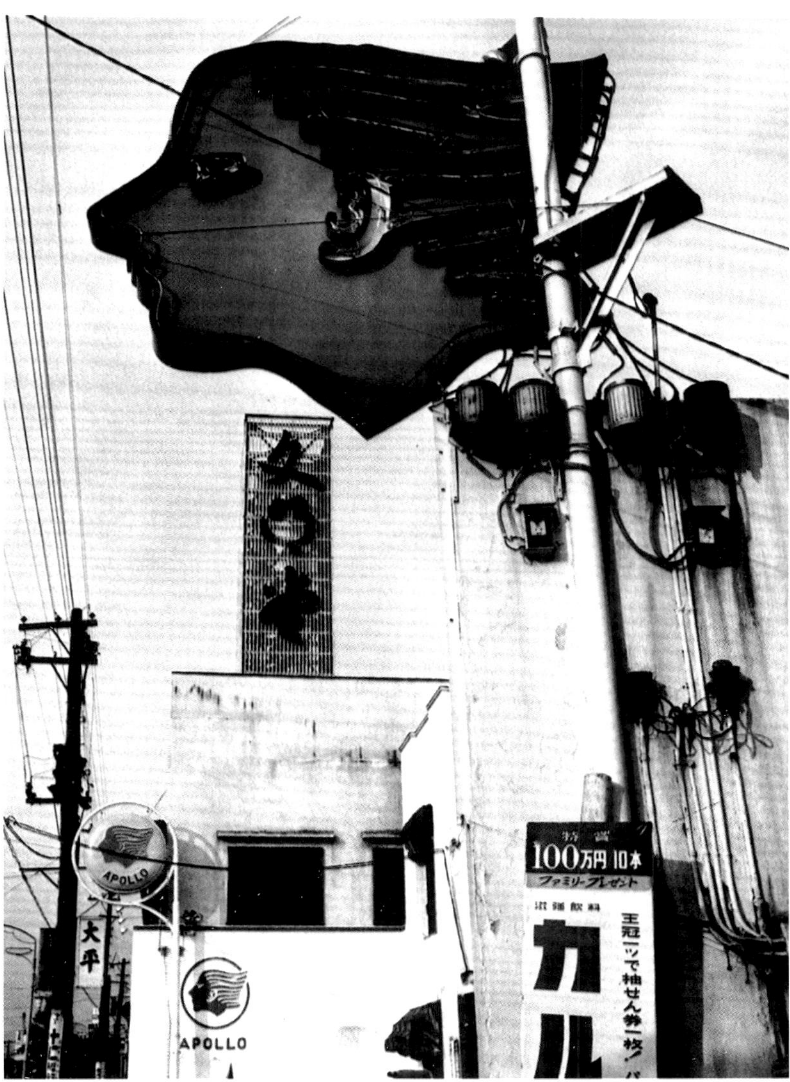
特賞
100万円 10本
ファミリープレゼント
王冠二ッで抽せん券一枚！
カル
APOLLO
APOLLO
大平

38. Hairdressing school, Tokyo, 1961.

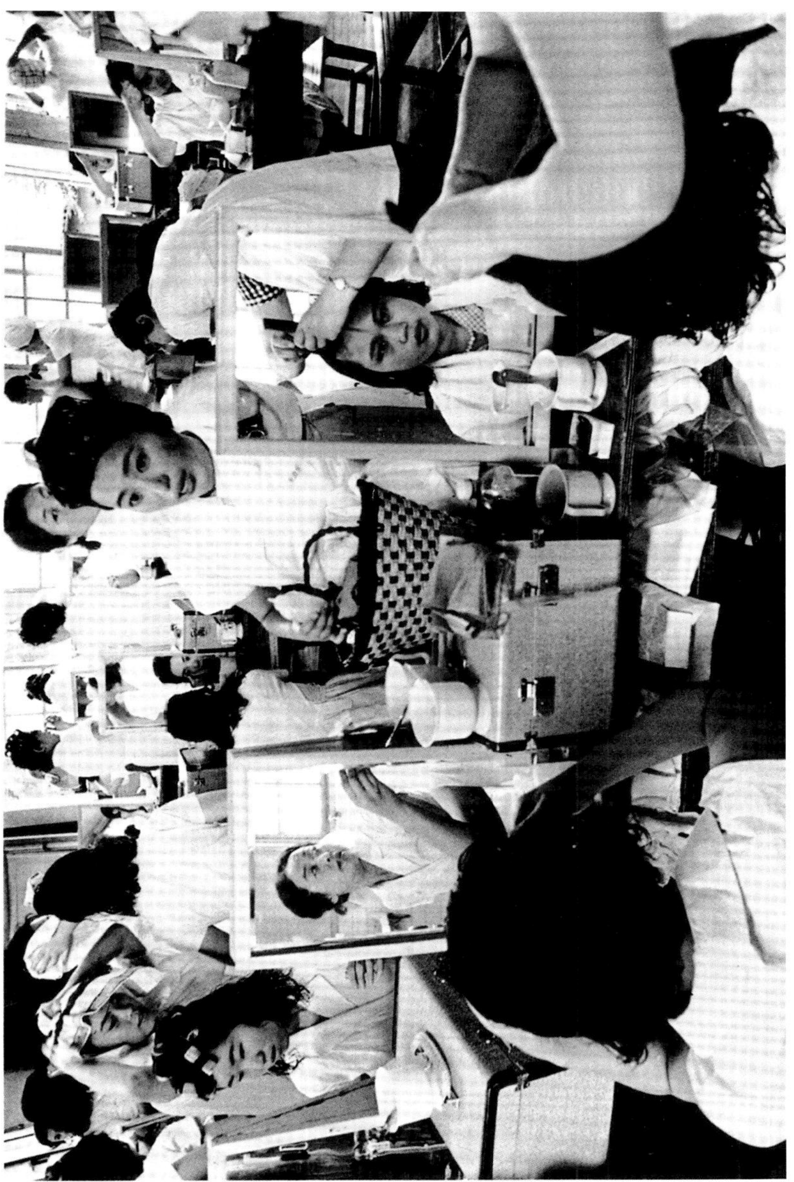

39. Metro, Tokyo, 1961.

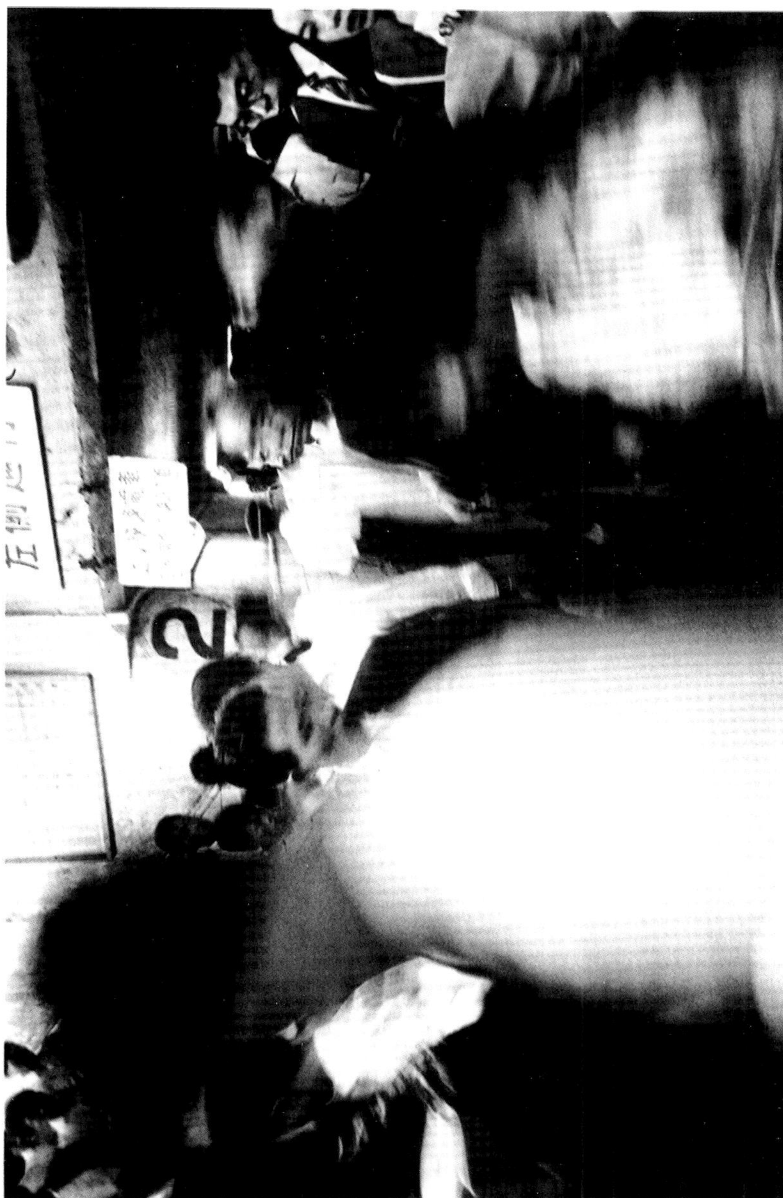

40. Confetti, Tokyo, 1961.

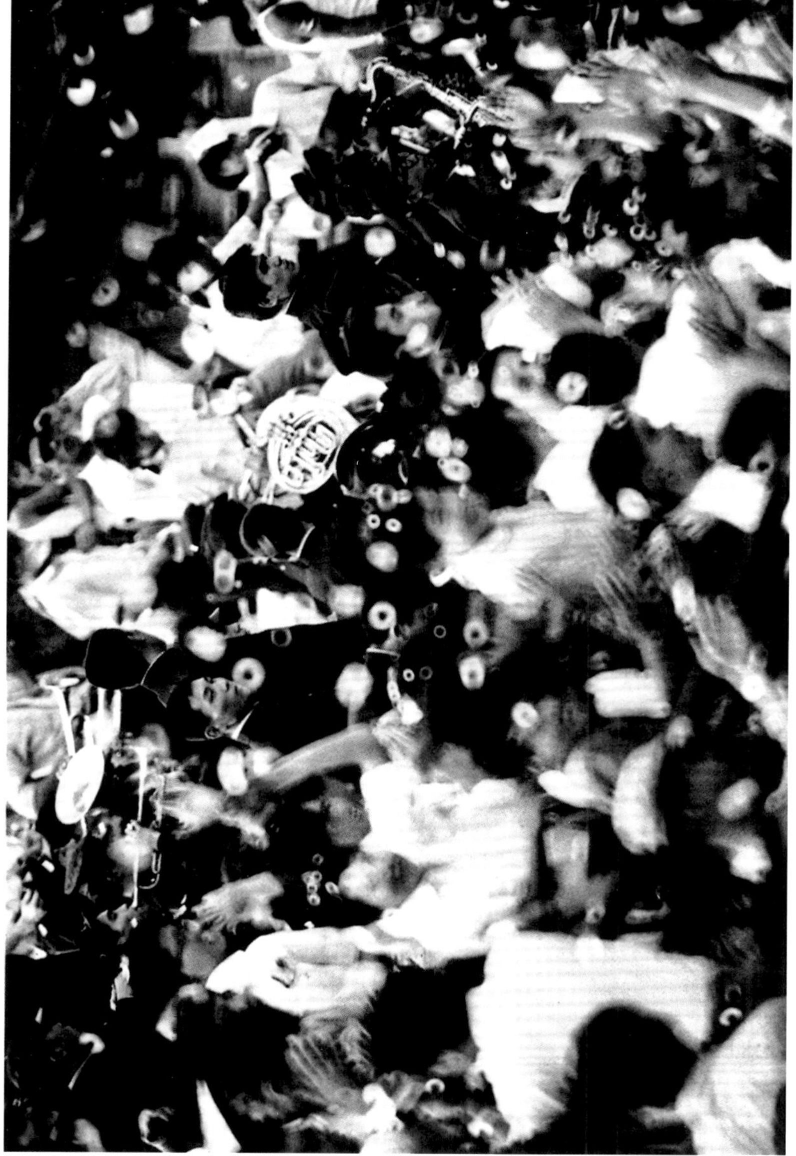

41. Santorini, Greece, 1956.

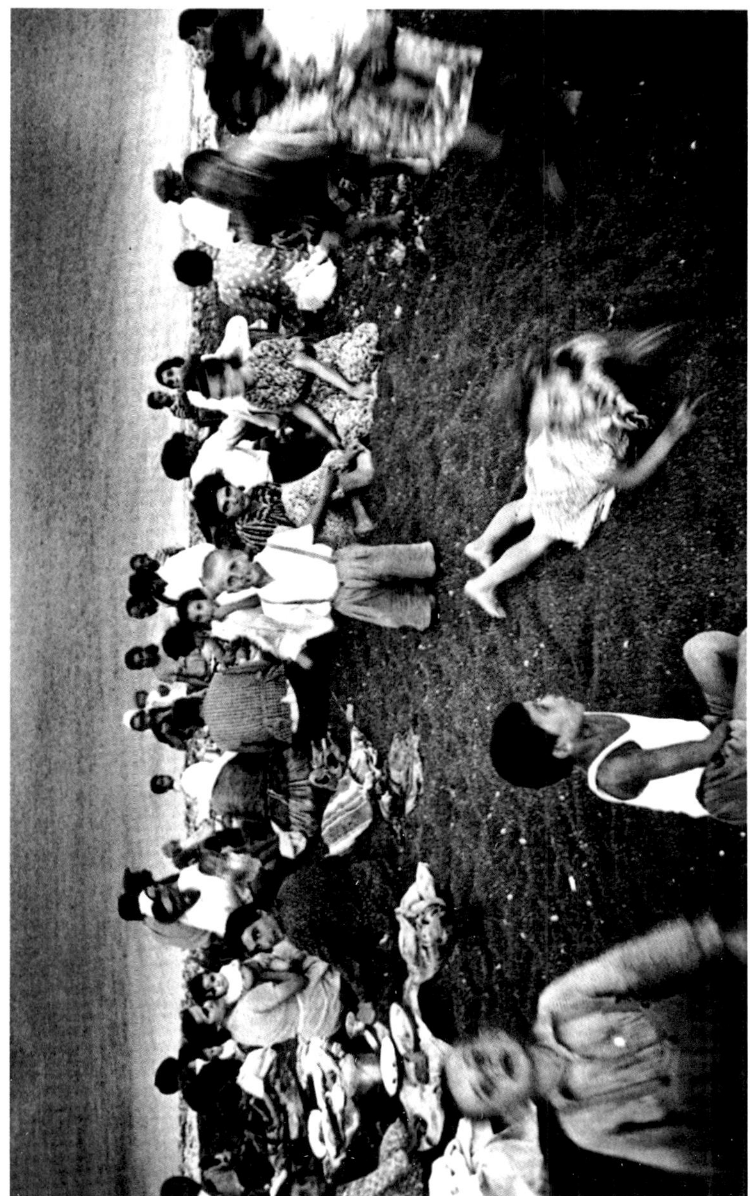

42. Metro, Paris, 1970.

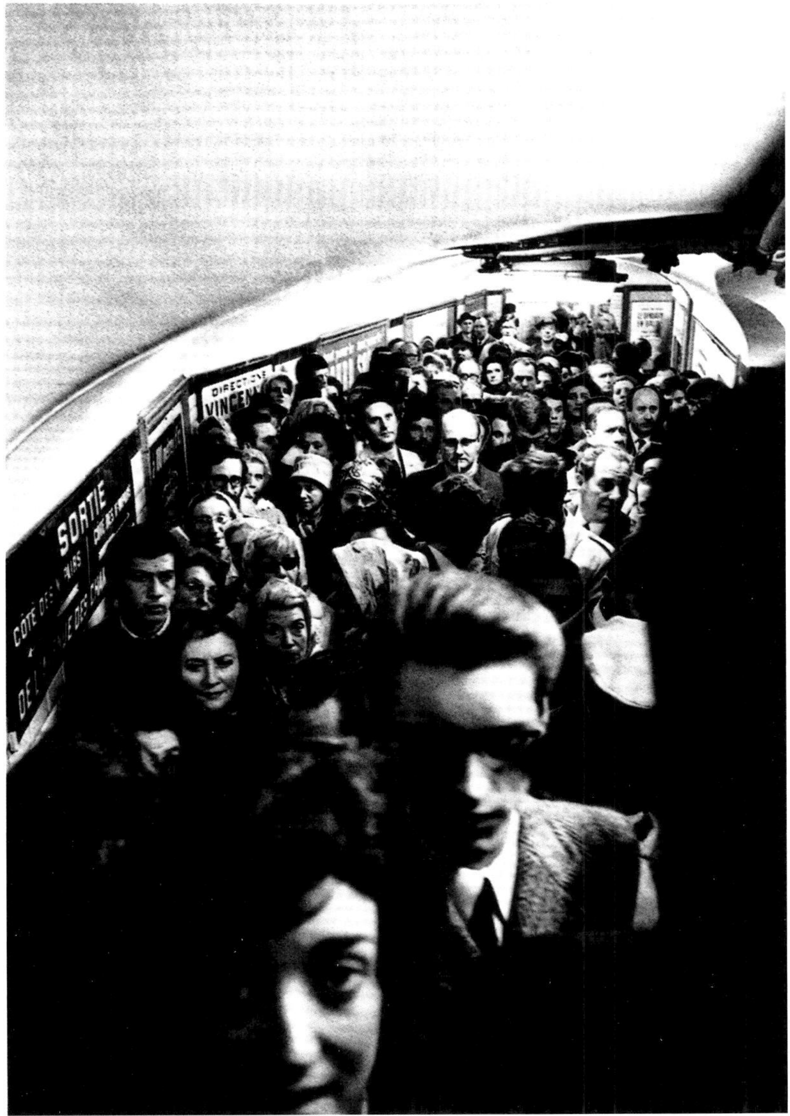
DIRECTION
VINCENNES
SORTIE
CÔTE DES …
DE L …

43. Mother and daughter, Paris, 1953.

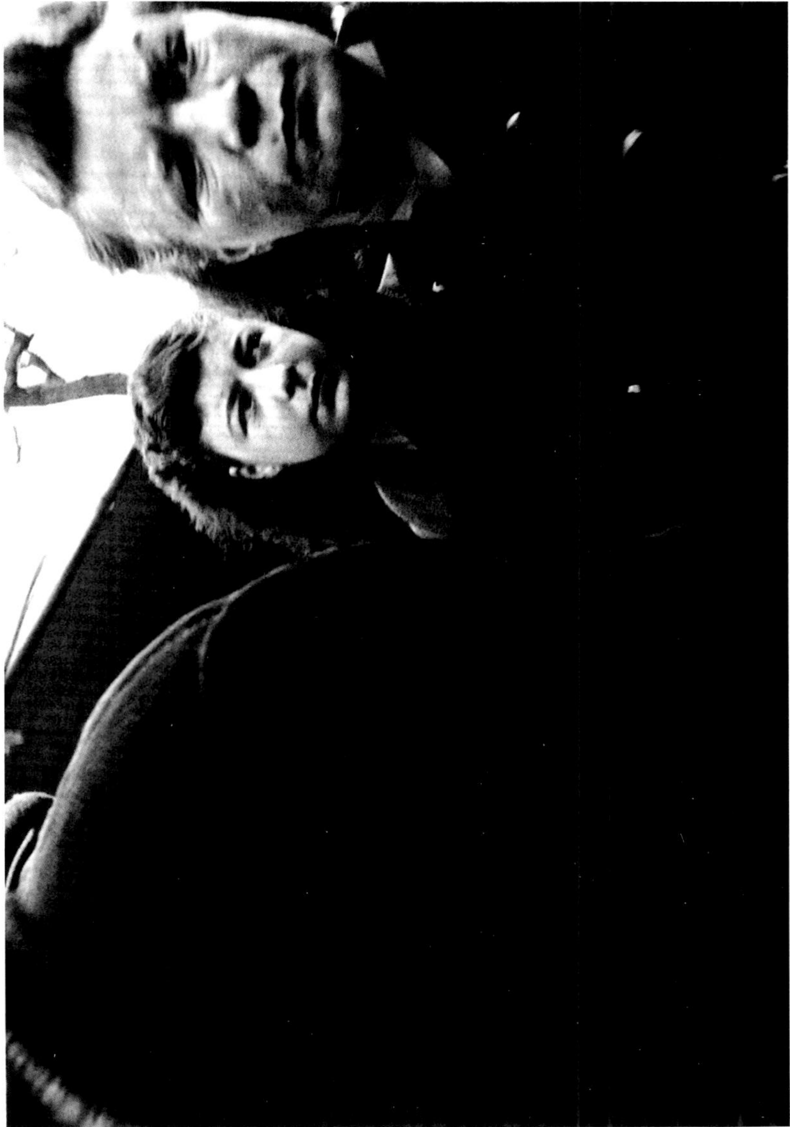

44. Funeral of Tino Rossi, La Madeleine, Paris, 1983.

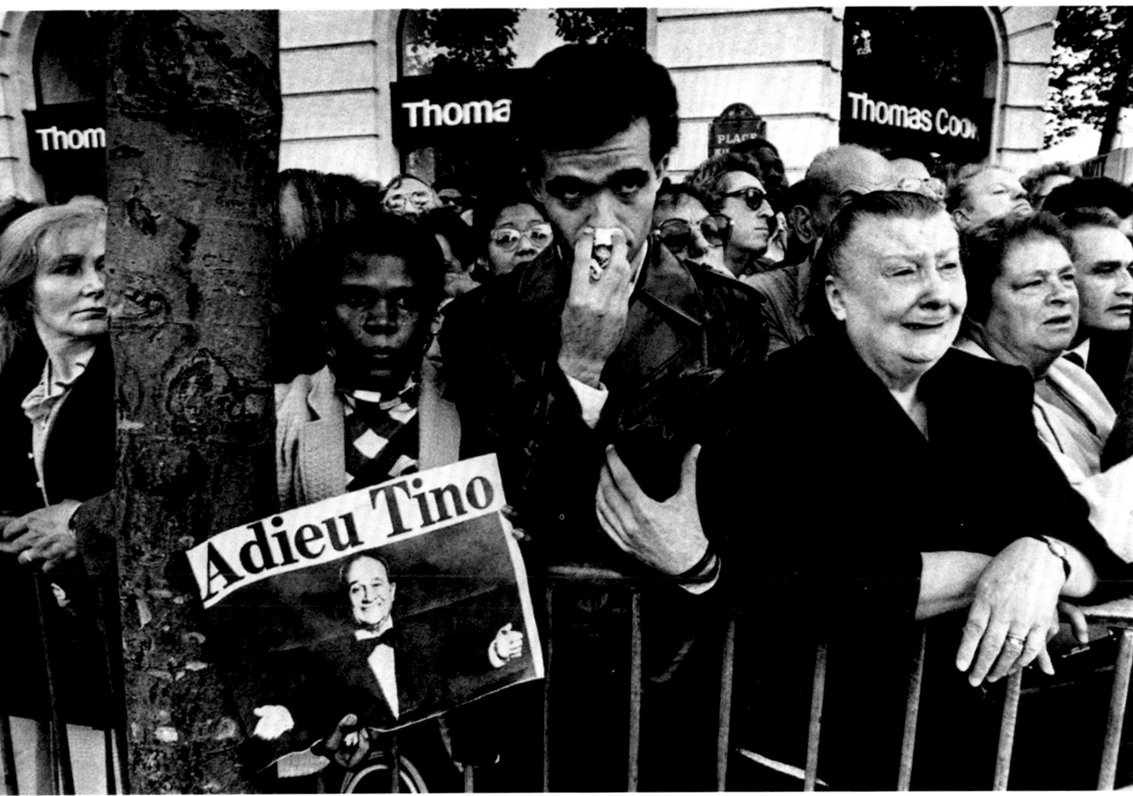

Thom
Thoma
Thomas Cook
PLACE
Adieu Tino

45. Paris Marathon finishing line, 1982.

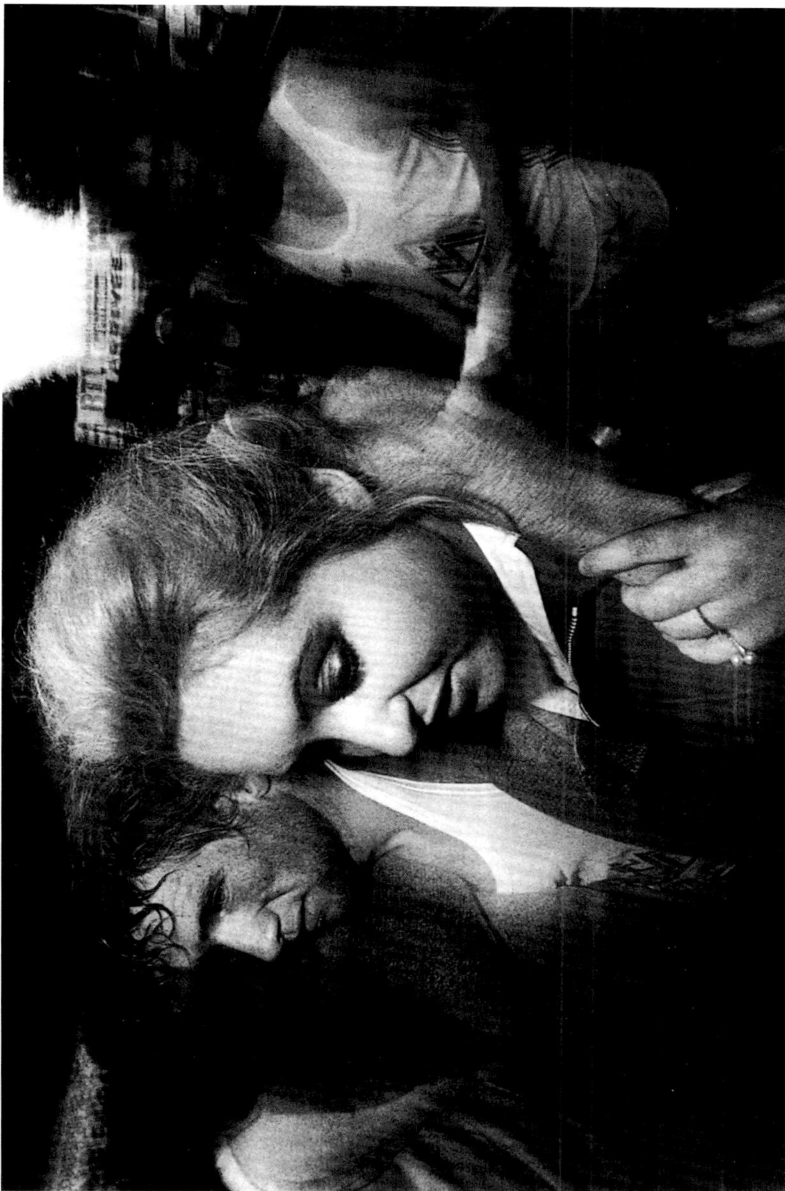

46. Funeral of Jacques Duclos, Paris, 1975.

l'Humanité

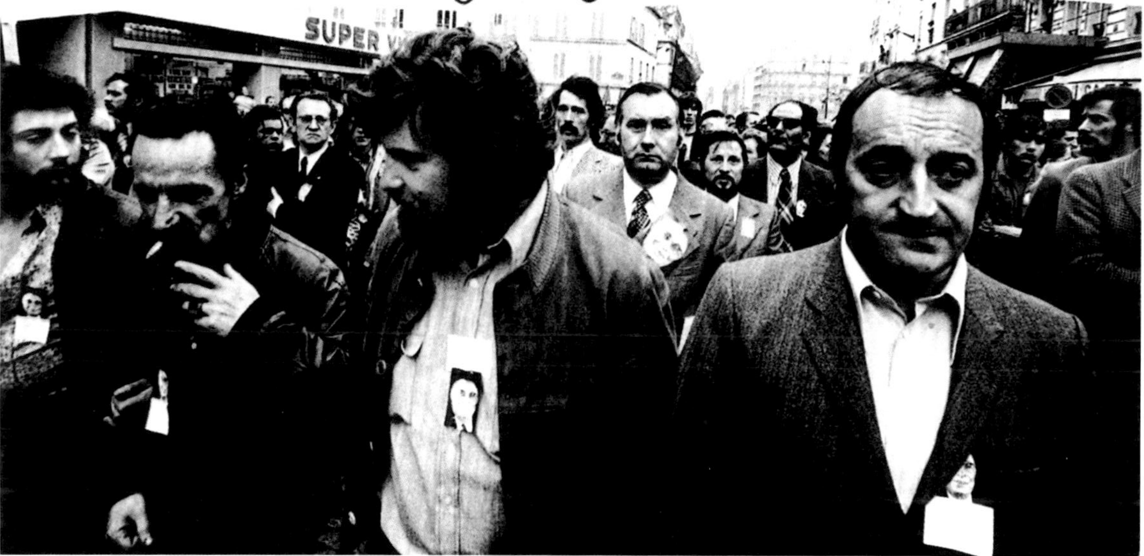

47. Funeral of Jean-Paul Sartre, Montparnasse Cemetery, 1980.

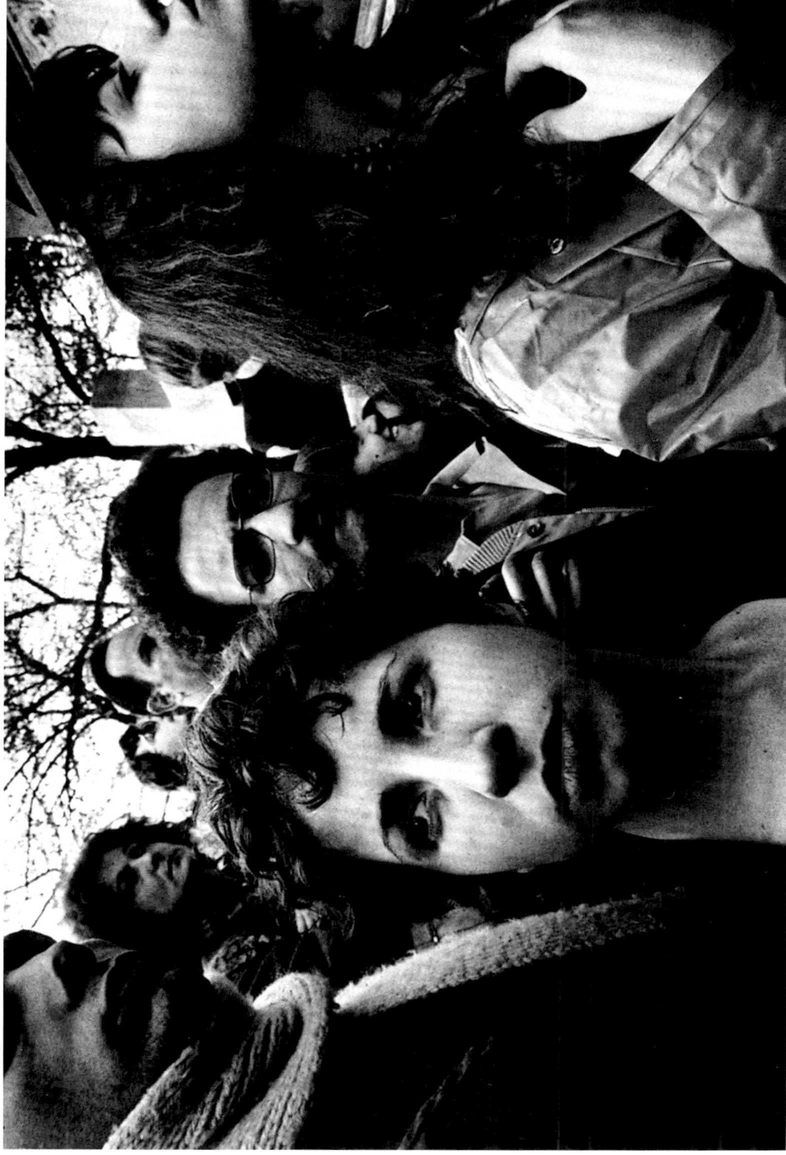

48. Café terrace, Paris, 1980.

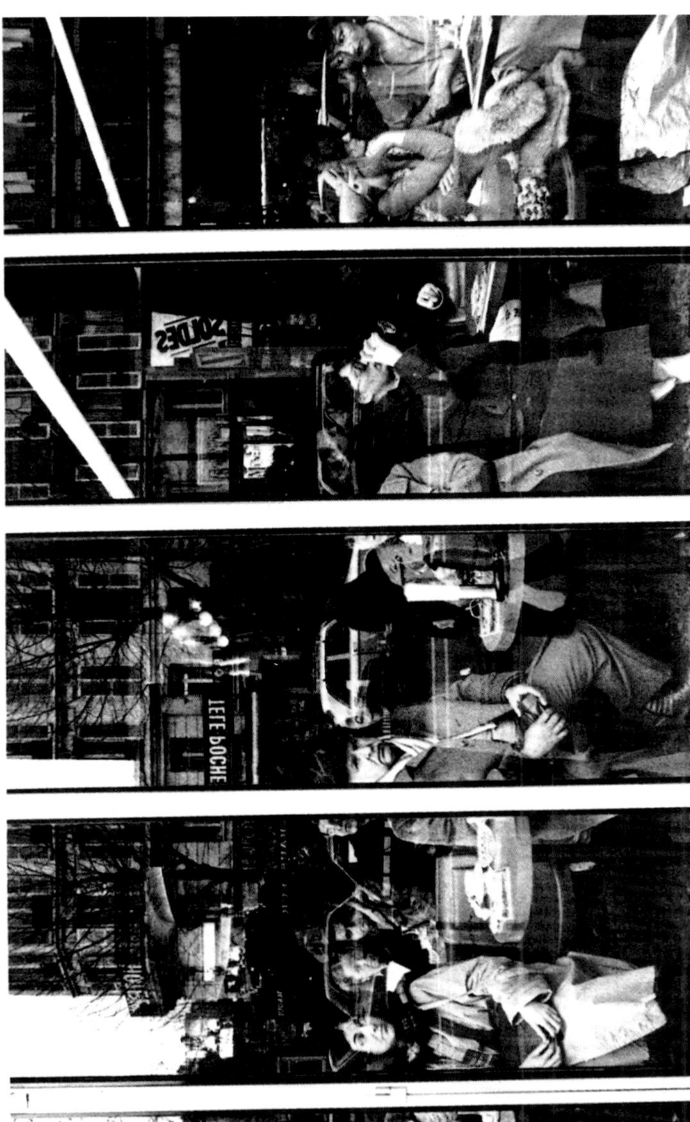

49. Canadian dance company La La La Human Steps
on the Paris Métro, 1992.

Overleaf
50 & 51. Monster Ball, Paris, 1982.

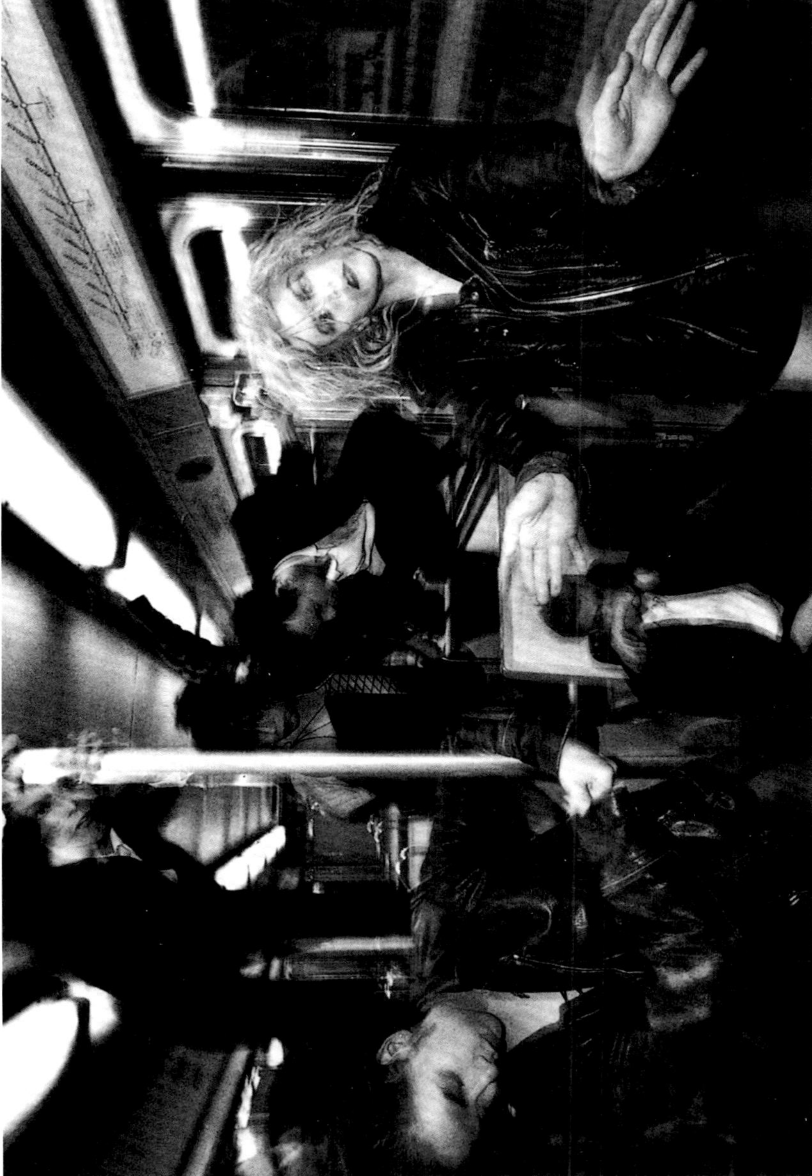

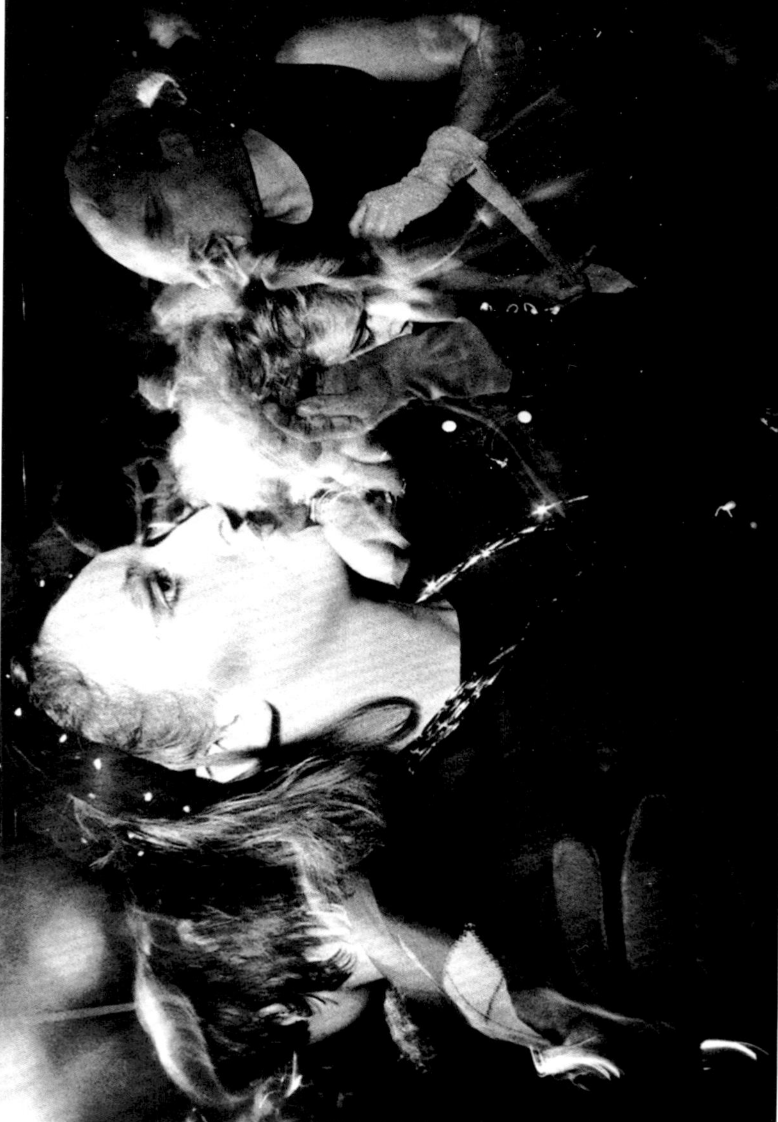

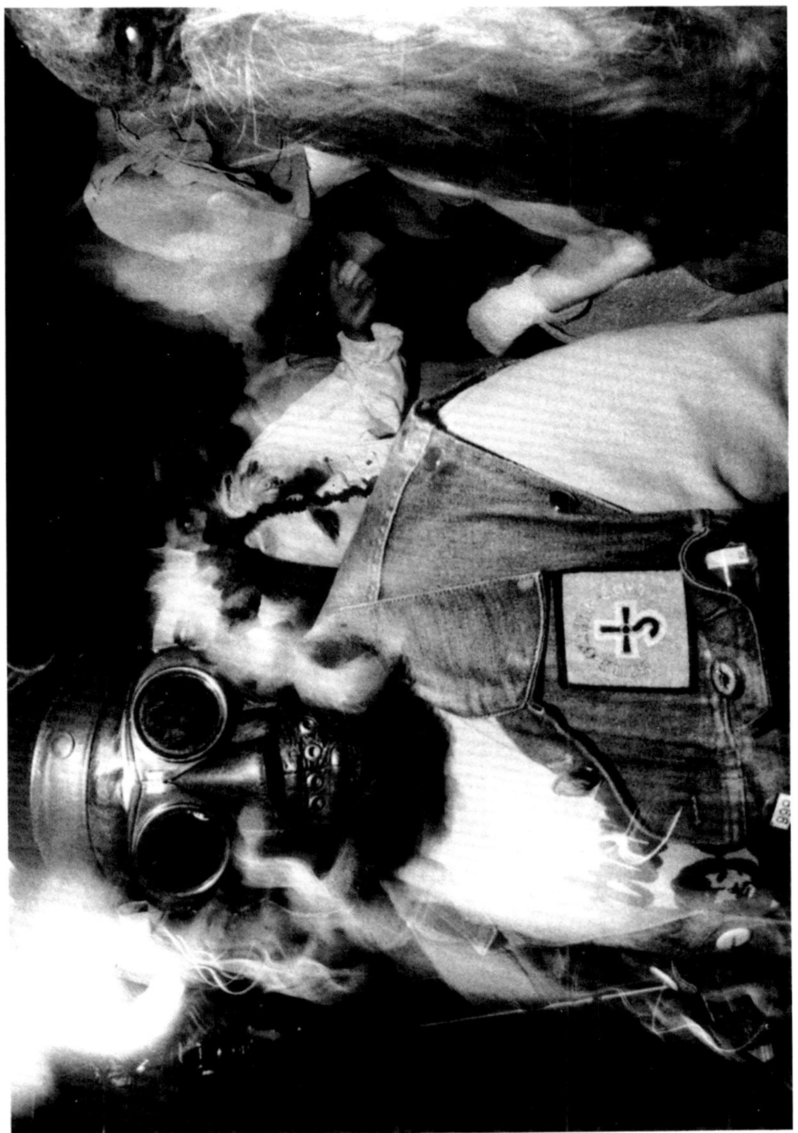

52. Backstage, Jean Paul Gaultier, Paris, 1984.

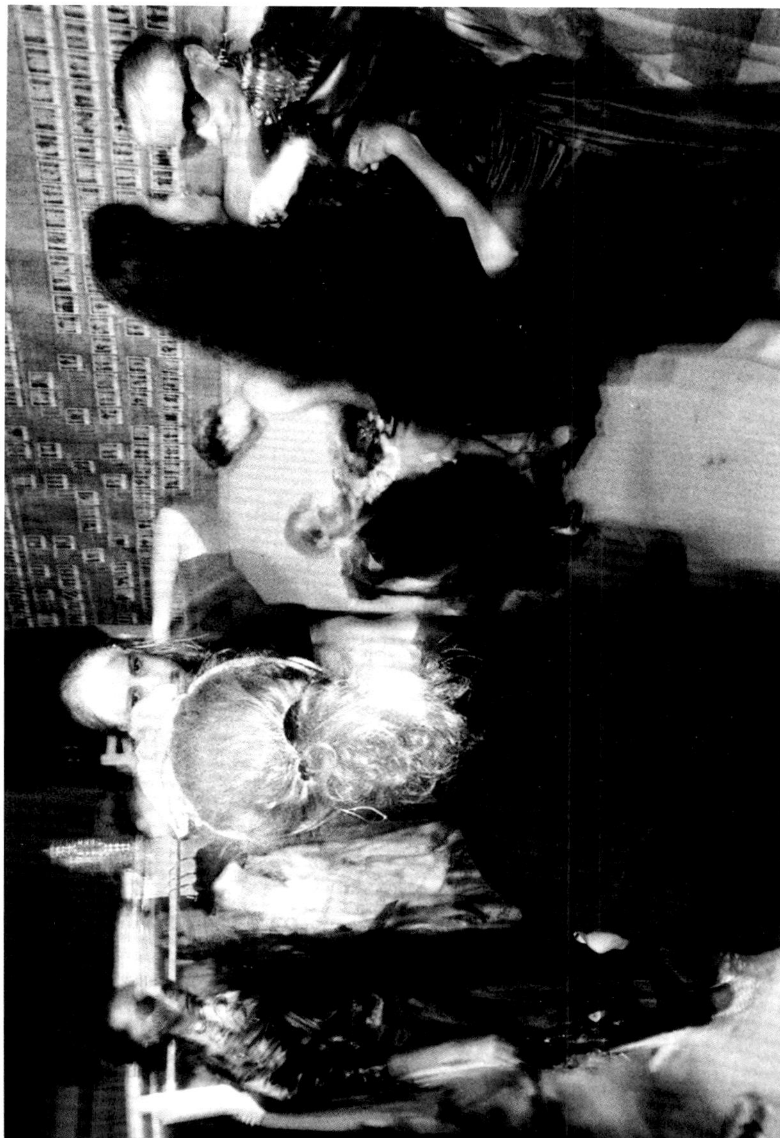

53. Rolling Stones concert, Longchamp, Paris, 1982.

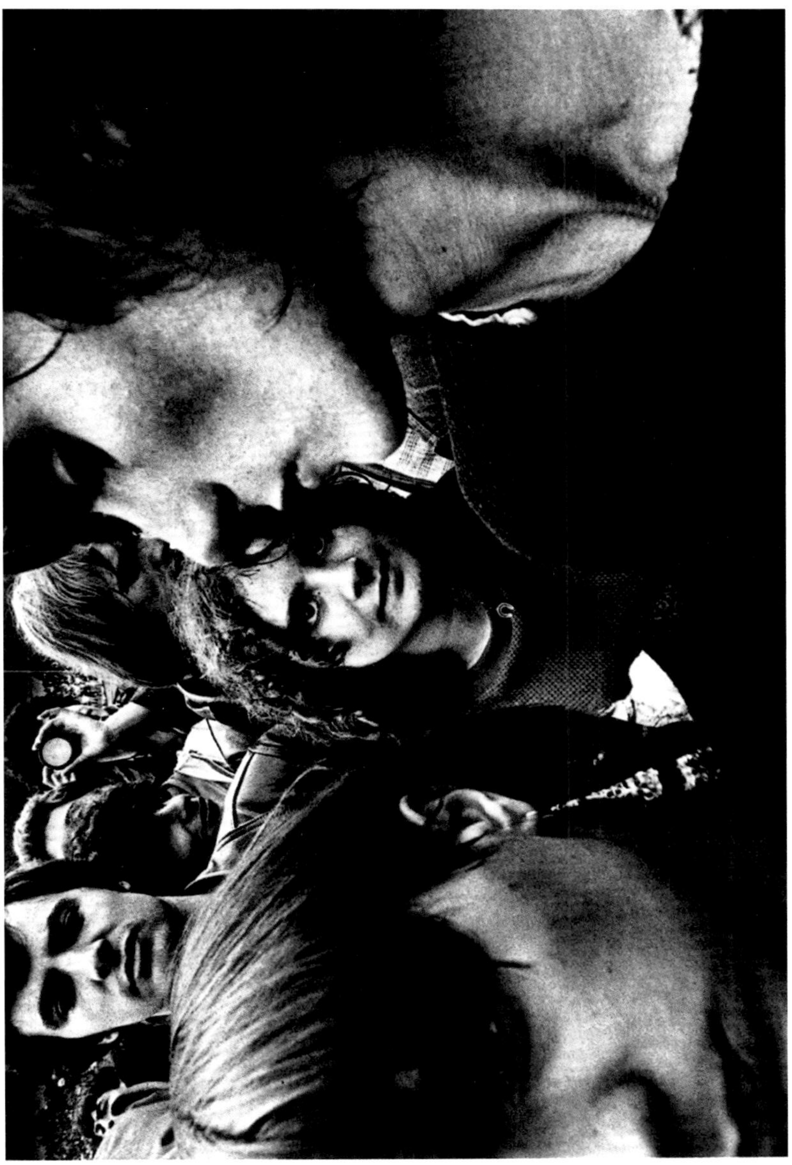

54. William Klein in his studio with his son Pierre, Paris, 1964.

Overleaf
55. Musée Grévin, *Vogue*, Paris, 1962.
56. Isabella + Opéra + blank faces, *Vogue*, Paris, 1963.

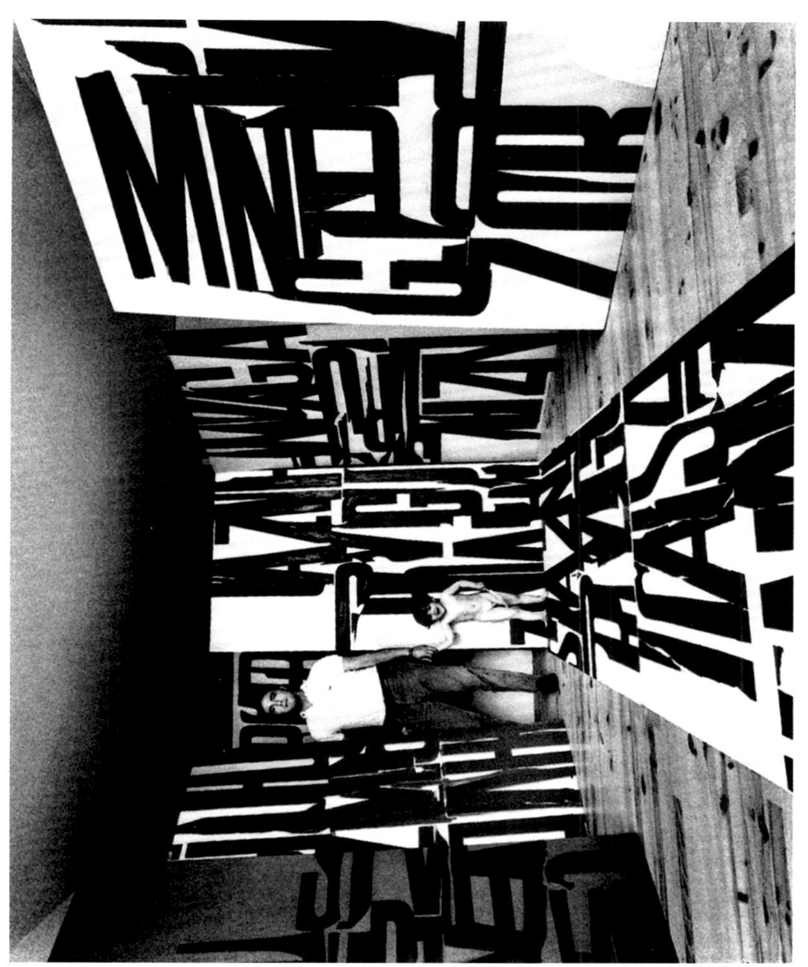

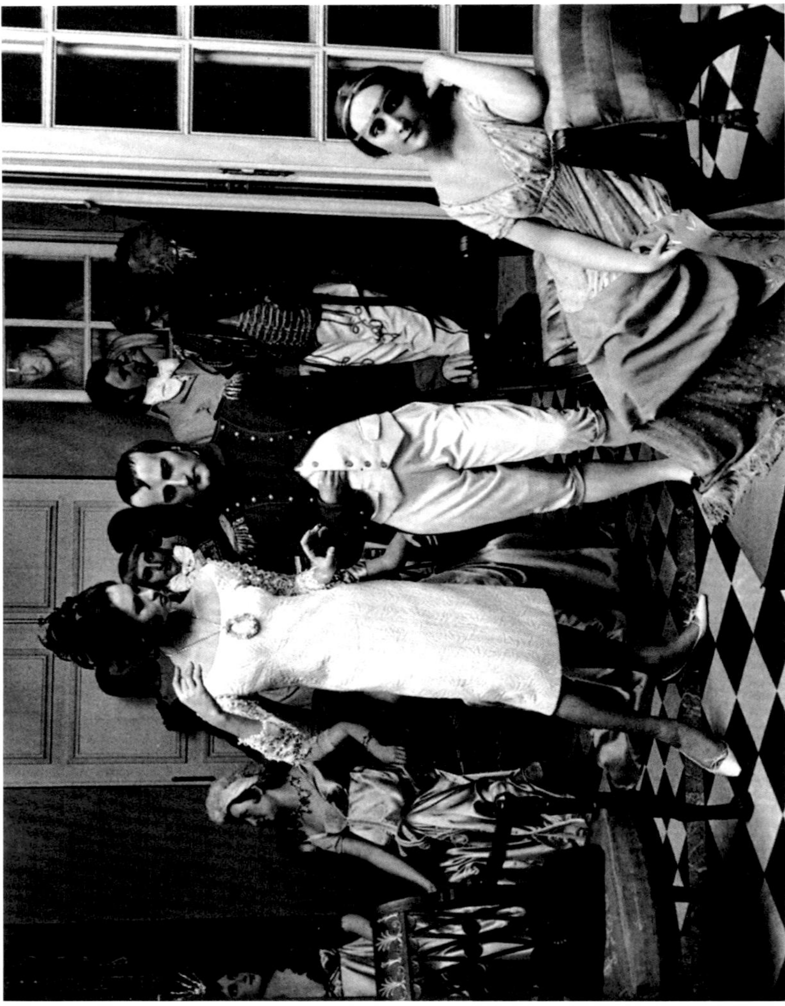

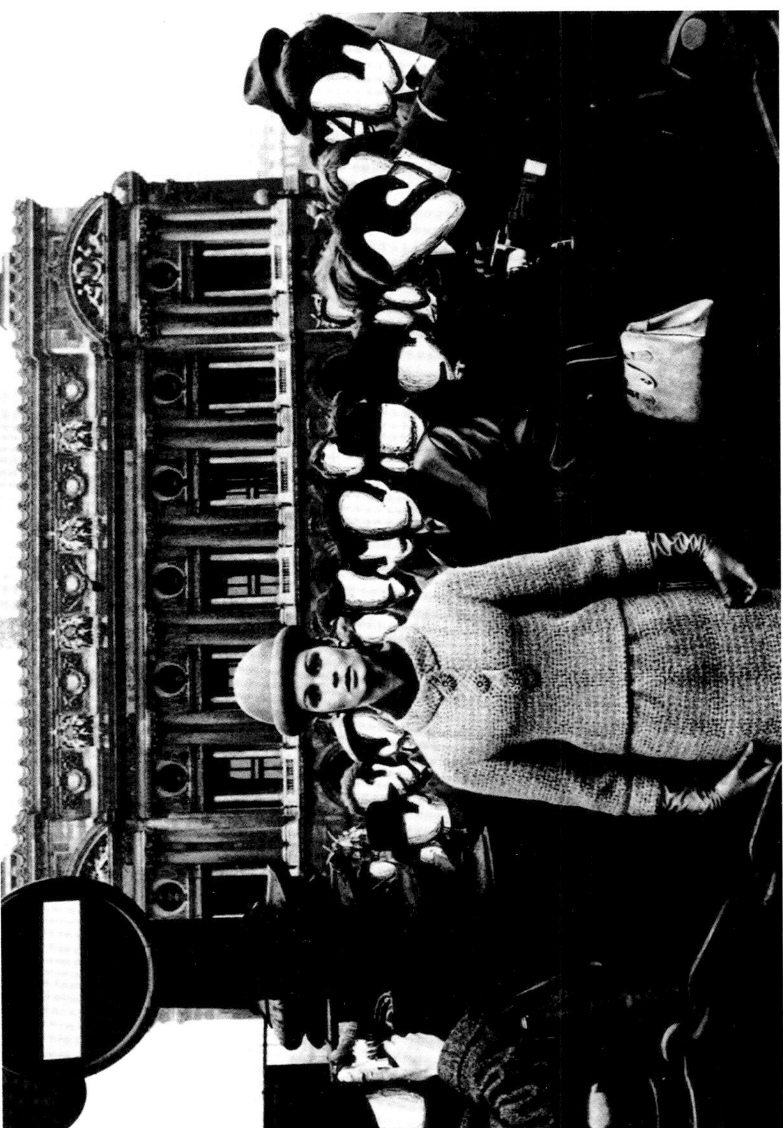

A note on Klein's painted contact sheets

When Klein takes his contact sheets and marks them up heavily
in primary shades of red, yellow and blue, he is transforming
the traditional process of photo editing into a form of artistic
intervention, but he is still making us think about photography.
He is underlining, in the most literal sense, the fact that the act
of choosing one image from the many that have been taken is a
fundamental part of building up a text. Like the rebellious boy he is,
he takes the opposite approach to his predecessors, who refused to
display the 'rough drafts' of their contact sheets, and so transforms
photography in its most raw form into a work of art. This process also
encompasses drips, crossings-out and other marks that both compete
with the chosen image and highlight it. A logical continuation of his
film work in which a narrative camera pans over contact sheets, these
painted images reflect Klein's irreverent attitude to the medium itself,
while also serving as an an affirmation of his endless quest for graphic
effectiveness. It is as if, for him, photography always requires some
kind of *mise en page*.

Christian Caujolle

57. Dance in Brooklyn, New York, 1955

Overleaf and following pages

58. Backstage, Issey Miyake, Paris, 1987.

59. Club Allegro Fortissimo, Paris, 1990.

60. Brazilian fans at the World Cup, Turin, 1990.

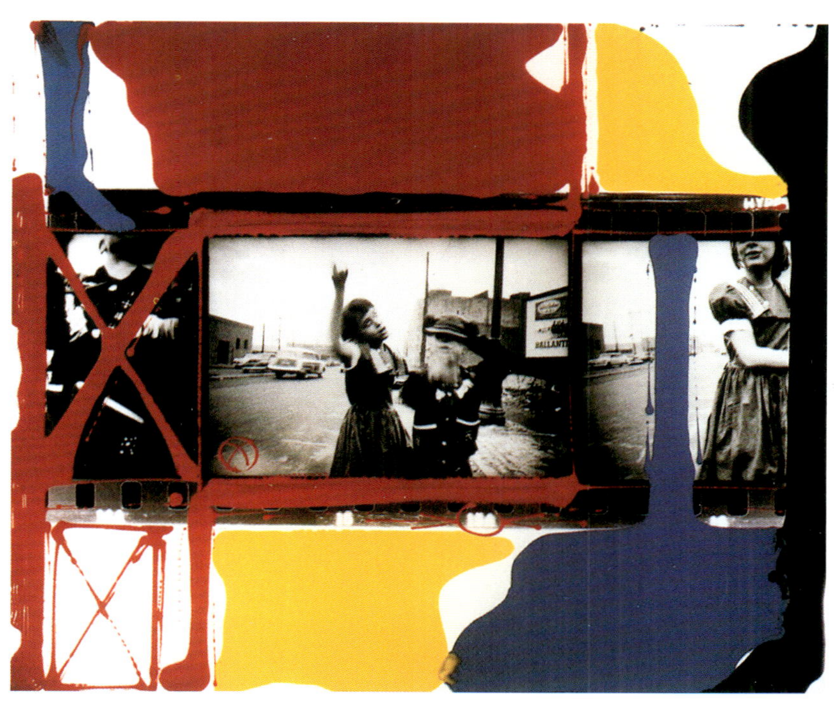

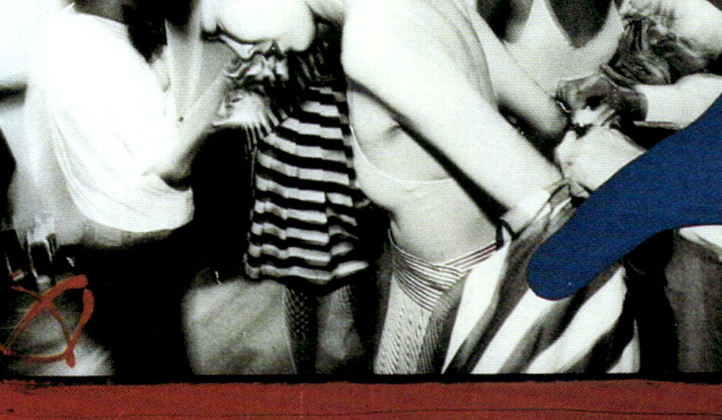

KODAK TM
- 15A
16

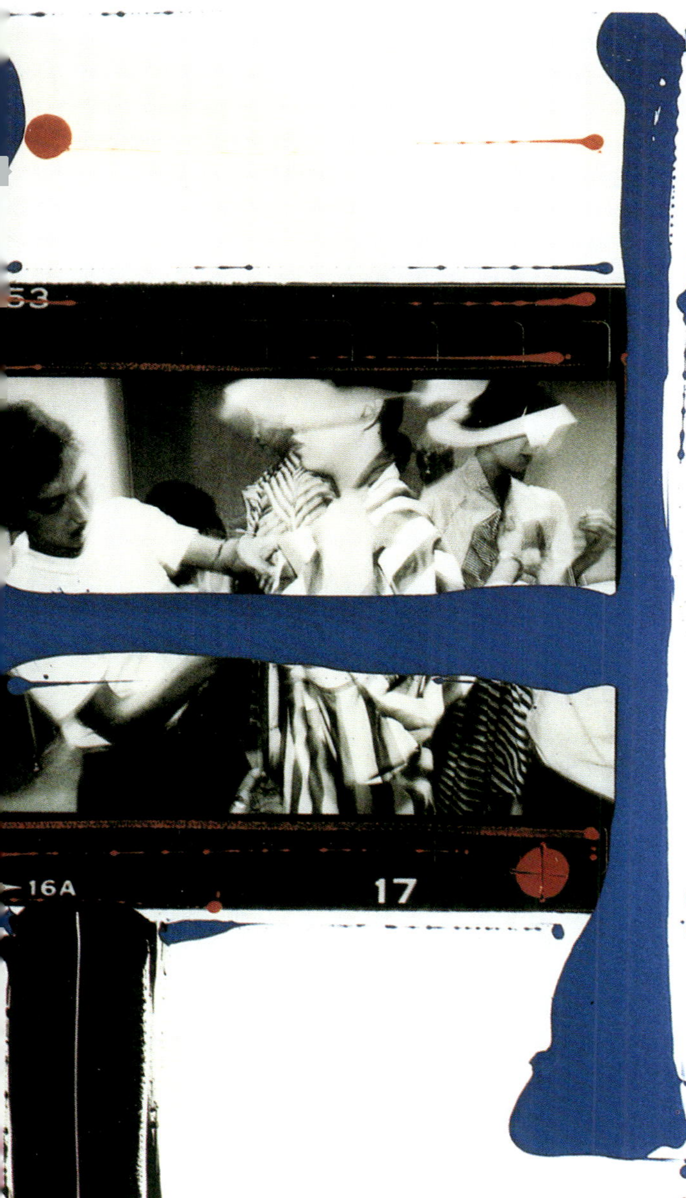

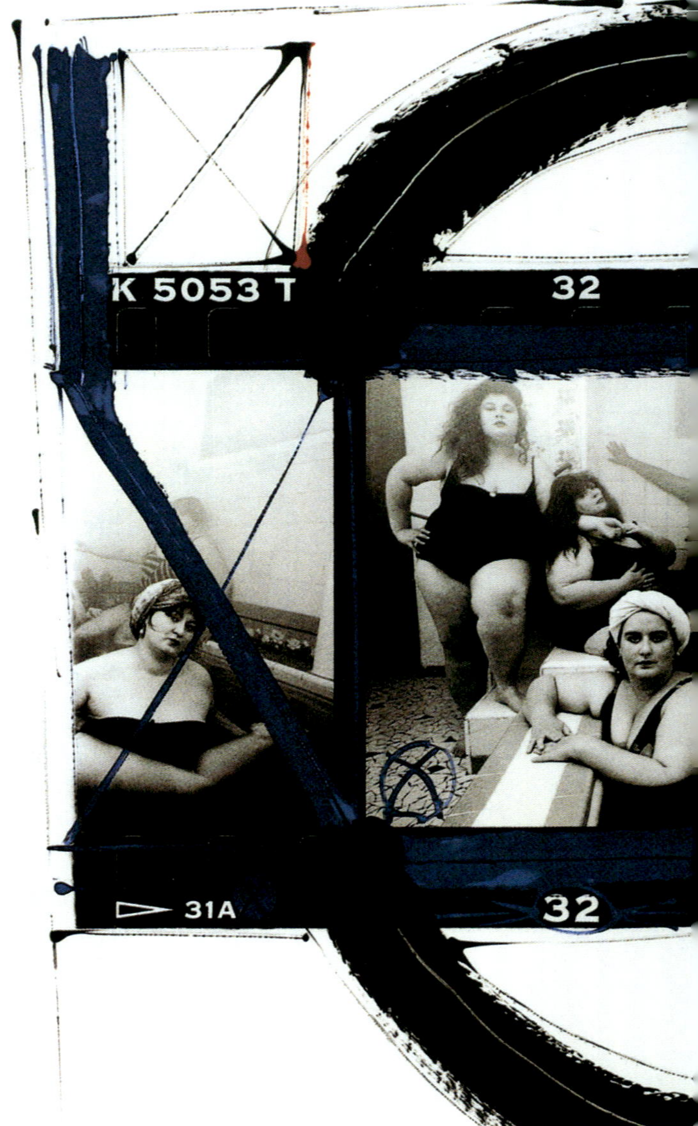
K 5053 T
32
31A
32

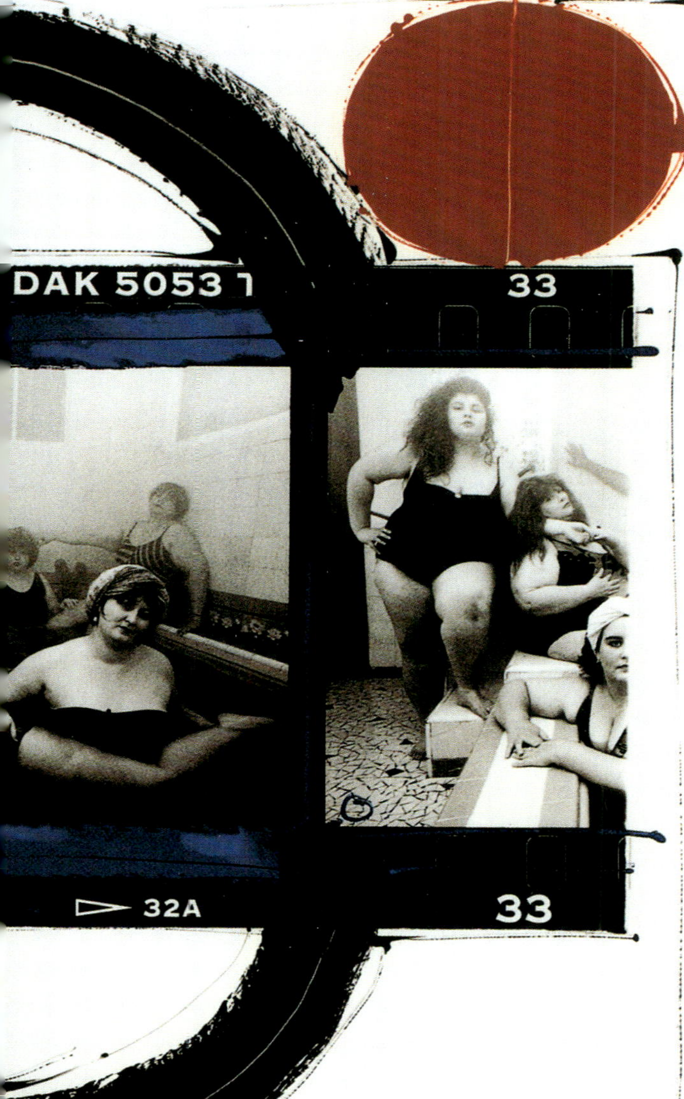
DAK 5053 1
33
32A
33

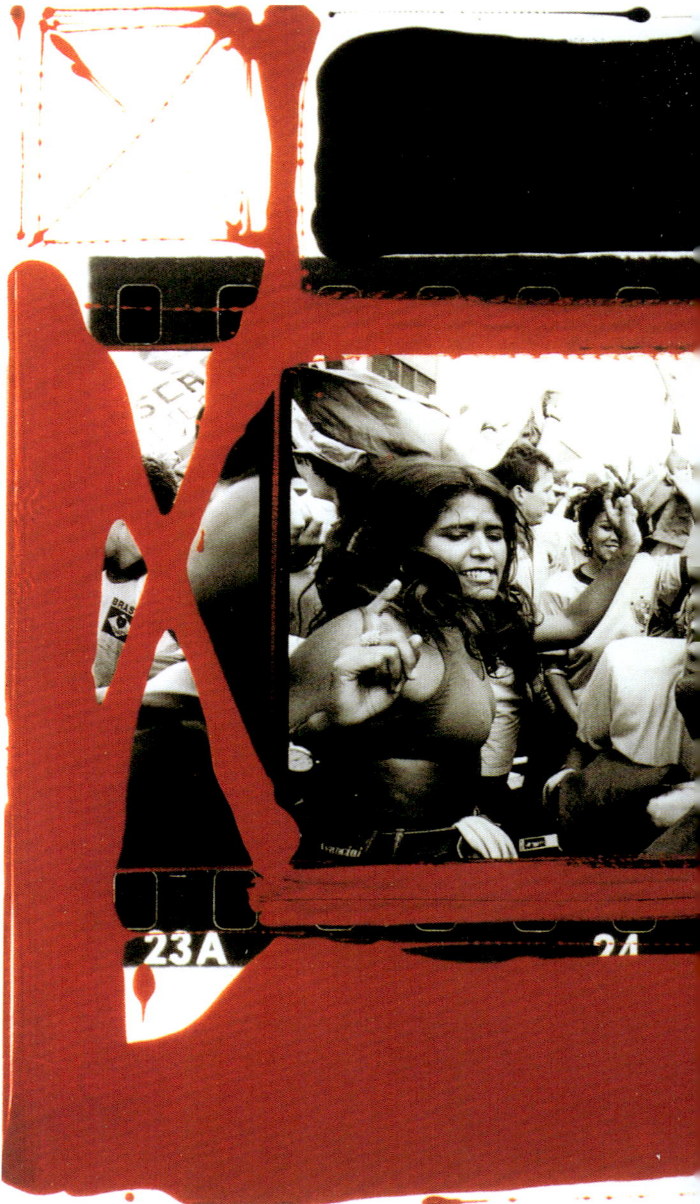

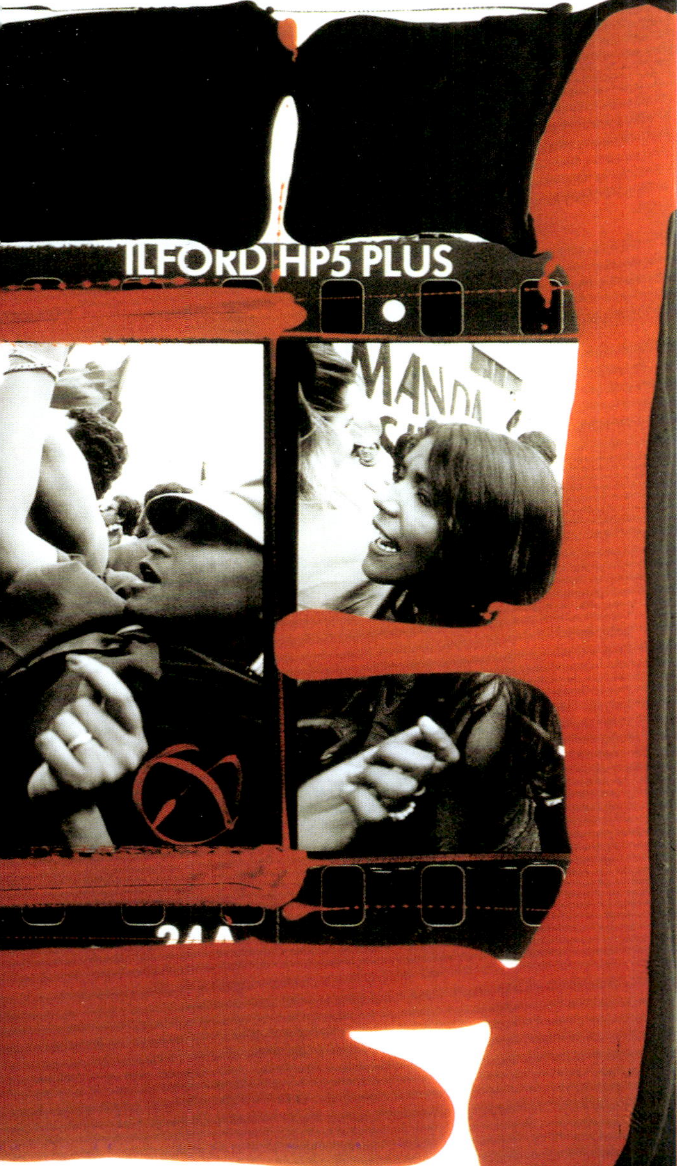

ILFORD HP5 PLUS

61. Constructivist dancers, 14 July, Paris, 1989.

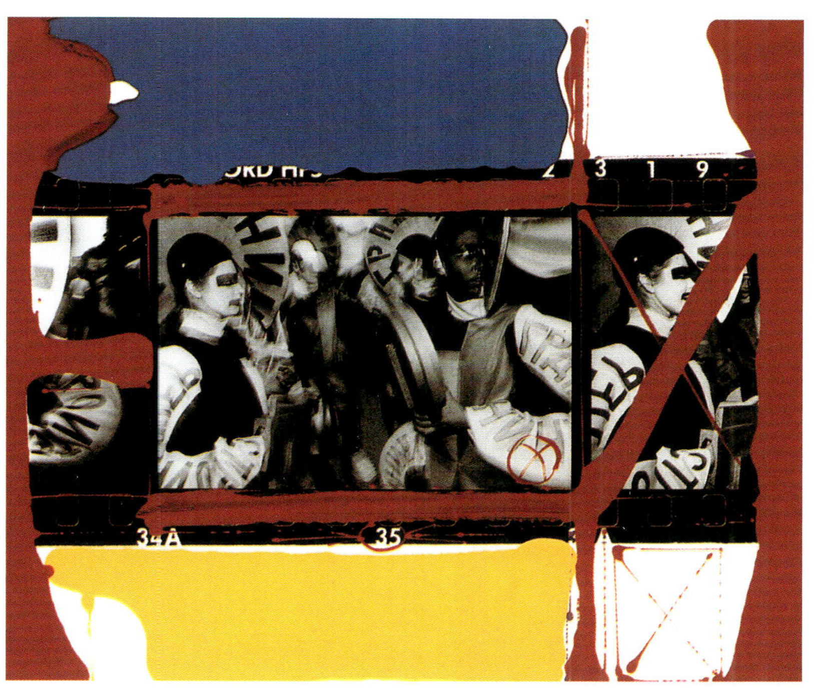
ORD HP
2 3 1 9
34A
35

62. Stills from the short film *Broadway by Light*, 1958.

LADD LA EVELY
ONN O'C
R A VD E TIE
ETWE E KI

VICTOR
G M ATUR
"G ZARA
COM ALAN FRE
CK HE ROC

TRACY
M VI IN"
OST RE W
E E"

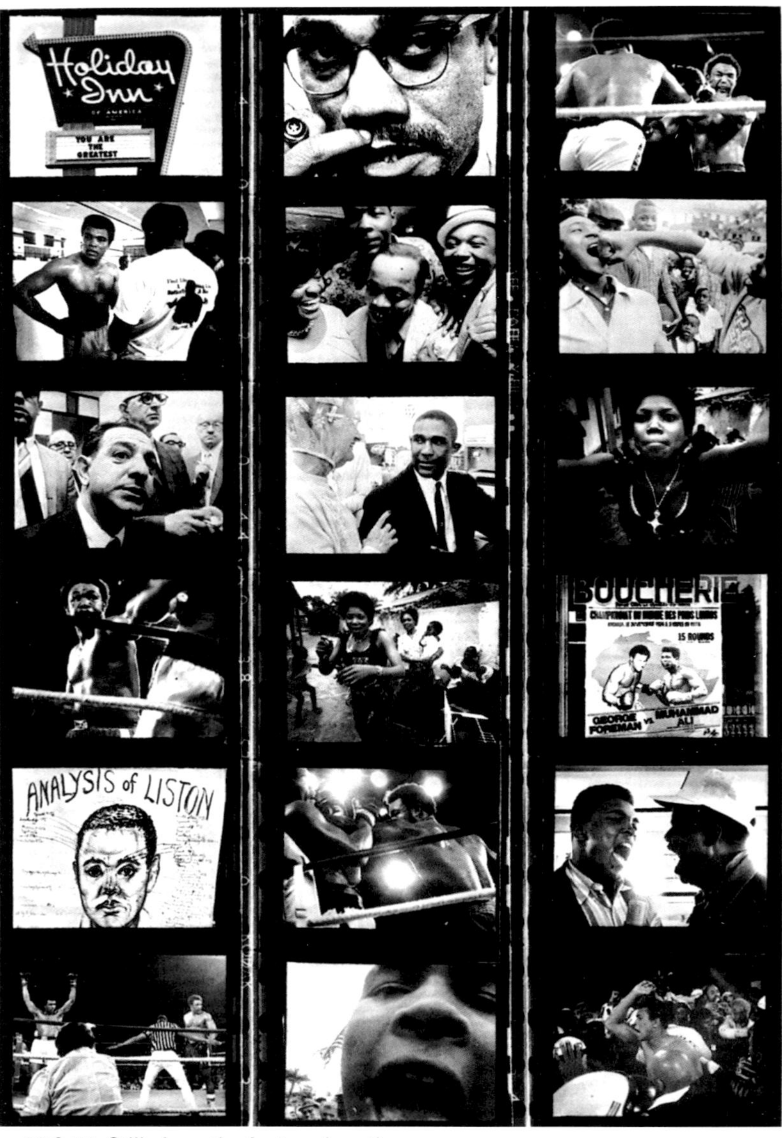

63 & 64. Stills from the feature-length
Muhammad Ali, the Greatest, 1964–74.

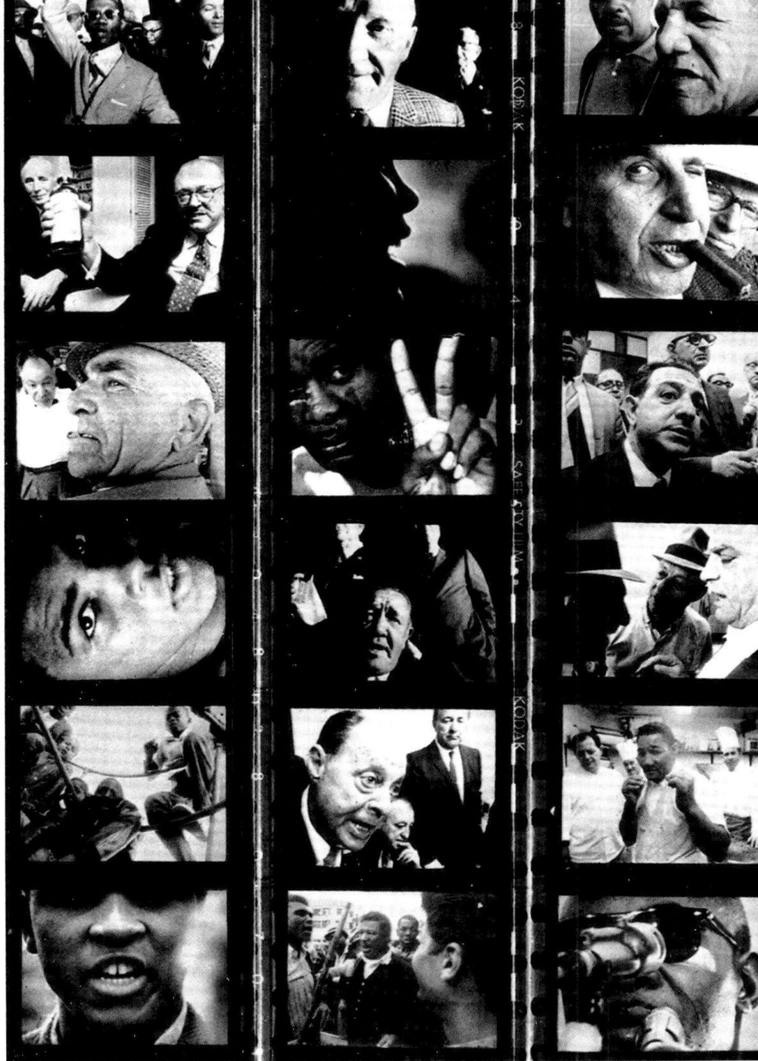

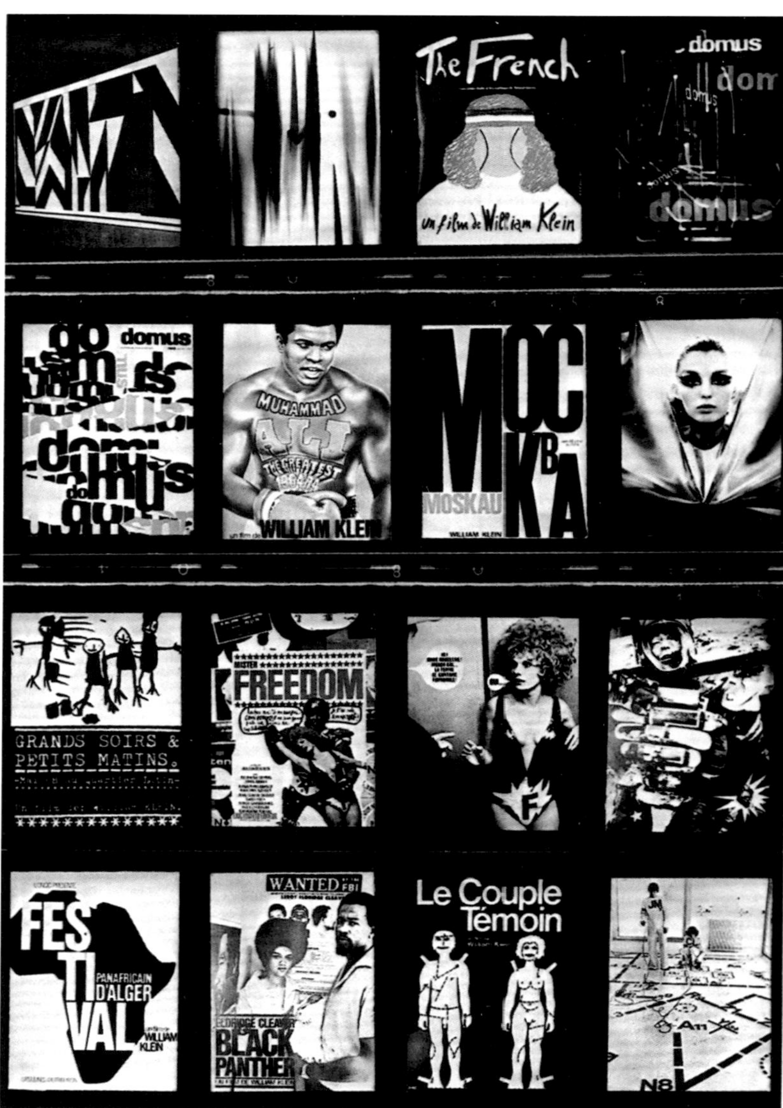

65 & 66. Drawings, posters and film stills.

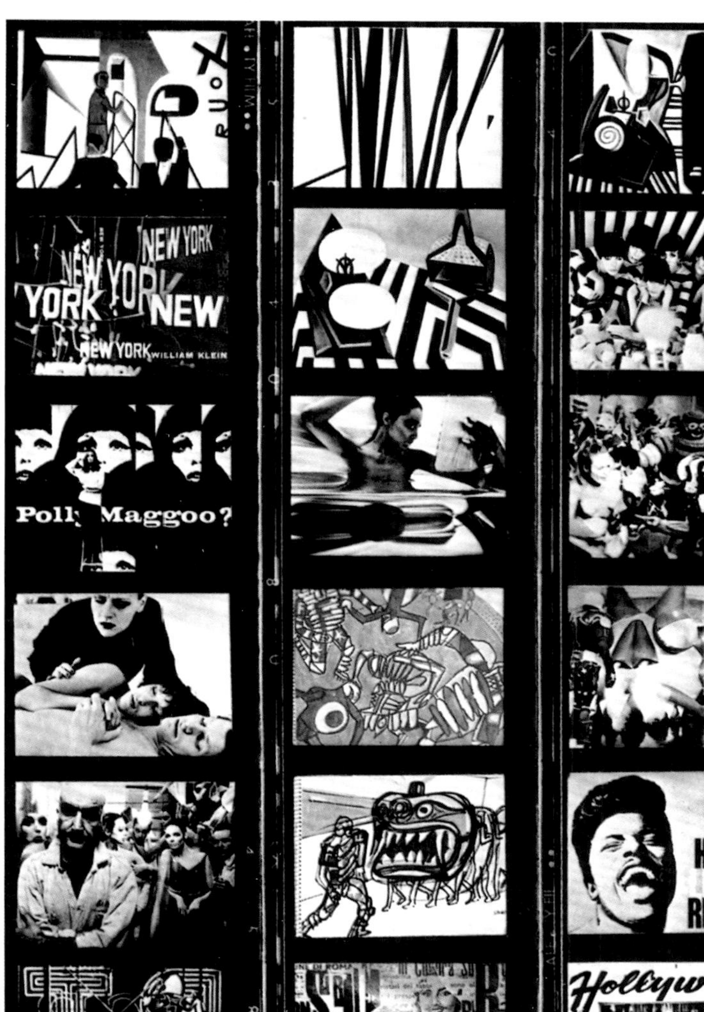
NEW YORK
NEW YORK
YORK YORK NEW
NEW YORK WILLIAM KLEIN
Polly Maggoo?
HERE'S
LITTLE
RICHARD
Hollywood
ROME
WILLIAM KLEIN

Biography

1928 Born into a family of Hungarian origin that settled in New York, Klein grows up there, studies sociology and does military service with the US Army: one year of occupation in Germany, one year at the Sorbonne in Paris.

1948–51 Demobilized in Paris, takes up painting and makes a rapid tour of the ateliers: a few days with Lhote, a few weeks with Léger. Not at ease in the atelier atmosphere, he withdraws to a Paris suburb. Marries Jeanne Florin, who remains his principal collaborator throughout his career. Through books he is influenced by the Quattrocento, the Bauhaus, Mondrian, Max Bill and more.

1951 Exhibition of geometric abstract painting in Brussels.

1952–53 Exhibitions in Milan at the Piccolo Teatro and Galleria del Milione. The architect Mangiarotti visits the exhibition and commissions a mural painted on rotating and sliding panels. Other commissions follow and he contributes work to the magazine *Domus*. While photographing the turning panels, Klein lights on a 'photo-graphic' idea: to fix on paper the patterns traced by forms in motion. Perhaps this offers a means of escape from the limitations of hard-edge painting. Following experiments in the darkroom, he translates some of his ideas into murals. Does a book of abstract photos and a series of covers for *Domus*.

1954 Klein learns of the existence of photosensitive glass in New York and imagines its application in architecture. Begins to blow up the photographs he has taken in his spare time. Why not follow the example set by Moholy-Nagy and Kepes in explorating figurative photography alongside abstract painting? Meets Alex Liberman, painter and artistic director of *Vogue*, who offers him a contract and financial support for research. Klein leaves for New York and works with photosensitive glass but fails to persuade Corning Glass, holders of the patent, to produce it on a large scale. He gives up the idea and devotes himself to a photographic journal about his return to New York.

1955 His New York 'journal' is offered to several American publishers, without success. In Paris, Chris Marker of Éditions du Seuil agrees to publish it.

1956 *New York* comes out. It provokes violent reactions, both for and against: this isn't photography, isn't New York, etc. But Klein is awarded the Prix Nadar. Fellini, having seen the book in Paris, offers him a job as assistant. Klein leaves for Rome, but the film is delayed. Might as well take some pictures for a book. .

1957–58 The album *Rome* is published. First fashion photos for *Vogue*. His first film – and perhaps the first pop film as well – *Broadway By Light*.

1959–60 Photos for the book *Moscow*. Shoots another short film in New York, and fashion photos. Works as artistic advisor on the film *Zazie dans le métro*.

1961 Invited by a Japanese publisher to do a book on Tokyo, and travels there via Moscow and India.

1962 Several films for French TV, including a series for the news show *Cinq colonnes à la une*. His 1½-hour programme 'The Frenchman and Politics' is censored – his collaboration with *Cinq colonnes* comes to an end.

1963 Shoots *Aux Grands Magasins*, with Simone Signoret, a TV documentary. His son Pierre is born. Participates in the exhibition 'Thirty Photographers of the Century', held at Photokina, Cologne.

1964–65 Publication of *Moscow* and *Tokyo*. He directs three medium-length films about Muhammad Ali, which later form *Float Like A Butterfly, Sting Like A Bee*. Writes and starts filming *Who Are You, Polly Maggoo?* Both films are produced by Robert Delpire.

1966–67 *Who Are You, Polly Maggoo?*, a film about media nonsense, fashion and other brainwashing, is quite successful and wins the Jean Vigo Prize. Klein virtually stops

taking photographs. He has the opportunity
to make films for the 'commercial' cinema.
But the Vietnam War is on, and he feels
that cinema's first priority is to denounce
America's intervention. He works on *Far
From Vietnam*, doing the American segment.
Writes and begins filming *Mr Freedom*,
a satirical comic-book movie about a
right-wing superhero.

1968 *Mr Freedom* is finished. Editing ends in
May but the film studios are on strike. Klein
joins in a project for a group film about the
Paris protests of May '68, which for obvious
reasons is never finished. Ten years later,
the footage becomes *Maydays*. *Mr Freedom*,
which the censor sees as a film about the
protests, is blocked for nine months.

1969–70 Invited by the Algerian government to
direct a film of the first Festival of Pan-African
Culture. Swept up by the current fascination
with the Black Panther movement, makes a
film in Algeria with Eldridge Cleaver. Both
films provoke great controversy.

1971–74 Participates in militant films and
experiments in alternative production and
distribution. Films life in a café for the TV
series *Les cinéastes témoins de leur temps*,
and another instalment of the story of
Muhammad Ali in Zaire. Tries to produce a
film about urbanization and the creation of
a city of the future.

1975 The screenplay about the city of
the future becomes *The Model Couple*.

1976–79 A series of films about America for
a German producer. More controversy, and
a number of commercials. In the US and
elsewhere, there is an explosion of interest
in photography. Klein's photographs are
rediscovered; a new photographic dialogue
seems to develop. Exhibitions, plans for
books, new photographs, especially in colour.

1980 A third film about an African-American
hero: *The Little Richard Story*. Exhibition at
the Museum of Modern Art, New York

1981 A three-hour film on Roland-Garros, the
French Open tennis tournament: *The French*.
Exhibition at the Light Gallery in New York,
and publication of a monograph by Aperture.

1982–84 Other books and exhibitions,
including a retrospective of paintings, films
and photography at the Centre Pompidou,
Paris. And for the first time, a series of
photographic commissions: *Sunday Times*,
Leica, *Libération*, etc. With the Centre
National de la Photographie, he conceives
a pilot for a series on the contact sheets of
great photographers. Film about slow motion
for the Musée de la Villette.

1985–86 A film coproduced by the French
Ministry of Culture: *Fashion in France*.
Exhibitions of recent photography in France
and abroad. Installation in the Palais de Tokyo
in Paris in the form of a labyrinth, 200 m
long. First edition of *William Klein: Photo
Poche* published by the Centre National de
la Photographie. Receives the Grand Prix
National de la Photography and is named
Officier des Arts et des Lettres.

1987–89 Exhibits in Tokyo and Osaka.
Monograph published by the Pacific Press
Service. Awarded the Kulturpreis in Germany
and a Guggenheim Fellowship in the US.
Several seasons of his films are held at
European film festivals. The Walker Art
Center, Minneapolis, organizes a tour of
his films in the US, Mexico and Cuba, and
publishes a catalogue. Finishes the book
Close-Up. Makes four short films for the
exhibition 'La traversée de Paris'.

1990–91 Wins the Hasselblad Award.
Exhibitions and catalogues. Touring
exhibition of Germany organized by the
Museum Folkwang, Essen. Exhibitions
in Paris and New York of new images
that combine painting and photography.
Photographs and designs a book on World
Cup fever in the city of Turin. Exhibitions in
Turin and across Italy. Retrospective of his
films at Film Forum, New York. Exhibitions in
Tokyo and Osaka, accompanied by a season
of his films and a catalogue. Films *Babilée '91*.

1992–93 Takes part in a group photography
project on the town of Almería in Andalusia.
Completes the editing of *Babilée '91*.
Exhibition at the Stadtsmuseum and Galerie
Mosel, Munich. Commission for the 500th

anniversary of the arrival of Christopher Columbus in America. Receives the AGFA Hugo Erfurth Prize. Cover and profile from the US magazine *Artnews*. Exhibits large-format painted contact sheets at the Printemps de Cahors festival and begins to design the book *In & Out of Fashion*. Makes a film of the same title featuring extracts from his feature films, photographs, costume designs and more. Oversees the printing of the book in Milan.

1994 Exhibits at Hamiltons Gallery, London, Zabriskie Gallery, New York, and FNAC, Paris, coinciding with the release of the book *In & Out of Fashion*. Retrospective at the Burgrave's House in Prague, at the invitation of Václav Havel. Paints contact sheets for the Southeast Museum of Photography in Daytona Beach, Florida. Exhibition at the ICP in New York to coincide with his new book.

1995 For the opening of MoMA in San Francisco, his *New York 1954–1955* images are exhibited in the US for the first time; 300 photographs, filling an entire floor. Designs a new edition of his *New York* book, with a third of the photographs previously unpublished. Shoots the Ilford calendar and a portfolio on the Fête de l'Humanité in Paris. Presents several of his films at the Virginia Festival of American Film in Charlottesville, and exhibits at the University of Virginia Art Museum.

1996 Makes a short film about the funeral of François Mitterand. Goes to New York for the launch of the *New York* book. Exhibition at Howard Greenberg Gallery. Takes photos of New York forty years later for several European magazines. Workshop at Fleury-Mérogis Prison, near Paris. Exhibition and book launch at Fundación Caixa in Barcelona. Major exhibition at the Maison Européenne de la Photographie in Paris.

1997 Retrospective of his films at the BFI in London and exhibition at Hamiltons Gallery. The exhibition 'NY' opens at the Fondazione Italiana della Fotografia in Turin, then tours Italy. For the 850th anniversary of the city of Moscow, exhibition at the Pushkin Museum of 250 photographs taken in the 1960s. Retrospective at the Deichtorhallen,

Hamburg accompanied by film screenings. Exhibition at Fundáción Caixa in Madrid. Commissioned to shoot a portrait of Madrid today, to accompany a series taken in 1956. Writes a film adaptation of Handel's *Messiah*, a work that has been adored, discussed, deconstructed and rediscovered over 250 years with the intention of making an 'oratorio for the turn of the millennium'.

1998–99 Records performance of the Messiah at the Opéra Bastille, conducted by Marc Minkowski. Designs and publishes the book *Films* on his cinema work. Exhibition at FNAC Saint-Lazare in Paris, then touring; films screened in Paris and around France. Exhibition of 'In & Out of Fashion' in Moscow. Exhibition at Scottish National Gallery and film screenings. Named president of the ARP Rencontres Cinématographiques, Dijon. Awarded the Centenary Medal by the Royal Photographic Society. Completes the filming of *Messiah* in France, Spain, Russia and the US. Edits film for release in France in December 1999.

2000 Season of his films at Harvard Film Archive and release of *Messiah* in the US, to critical and public acclaim. Screenings and retrospectives at festivals in Amsterdam, Sheffield, Prades (southern France), and at the Cinéma Racine, Paris.

2001 Takes part in the retrospective 'Les années Pop' at the Centre Pompidou, with *Broadway by Light*, photographs and montages. Exhibits painted contact sheets at Charles Cowles Gallery and vintage prints at Howard Greenberg Gallery in New York. With Robert Delpire, produces a book of photographs for Reporters Without Borders. Puts together a portfolio on the French Open tennis tournament. A season of his films is shown at the Porto Festival, as is an exhibition of his painted contact sheets.

2002 Photographs Paris in colour, in his view as multicultural as New York, for a new book, *PARIS + KLEIN*. Exhibition over two floors of the Maison Européenne de la Photographie, Paris, then at the Palazzo delle Esposizioni, Rome. Presented with the Medal of the City of Paris by mayor Bertrand Delanoë. A team from CBS film a profile of him for *60 Minutes*.

2003–4 Exhibitions of the work from his *Paris* book in New York, Milan, Berlin and Budapest. Takes part in a FIFA project to take portraits of the world's 100 greatest living footballers: he photographs Pelé, Cantona, Thuram, Del Piero and more. Group exhibition at the Royal Academy, London. Commissioned to create an exhibition and catalogue for the Transphotographiques festival in Lille; takes group portraits of people from the region. Open-air screening of *Messiah* in Dublin. Wins the Grand Prize at the Moscow Photography Biennale.

2005 Commissioned by Fendi and the publisher Contrasto to create a portrait of Rome, which becomes the book and exhibition *MMV Romani*, featuring group portraits of Rome's people. Wins PhotoEspaña award. Retrospective of photographs, paintings and films at the Centre Pompidou, Paris. His wife Jeanne dies in Paris, bringing a shared life lasting more than 50 years to an end.

2006 Exhibition at the Centre Pompidou closes, after a record-breaking 3,000 visitors per day. Makes a film about the exhibition. President of the jury at the Las Palmas film festival. Takes part in a group project about the 2005 riots in the Paris suburb of Clichy-sous-Bois, which becomes a book and an exhibition.

2007 John Galliano uses painted contact sheets in an ad campaign and is successfully sued by Klein for plagiarism. Takes photographs in Egypt for a new book: *Anywhere*. At the request of *Harper's Bazaar*, he shoots a portfolio on contemporary fashion designers. The city of Rome wishes to publish a new edition of his 1956 book, which is launched by the publisher Contrasto along with an accompanying exhibition. Receives the ICP Lifetime Achievement award in New York. Takes part in the Thessaloniki Film Festival, with screenings and exhibitions at the Macedonian Museum of Contemporary Art.

2008 For the 40th anniversary of the Paris protests of May '68, his film *Maydays* is screened on TV and in some 50 locations in France and abroad, including Lincoln Center, New York. Guest of honour at the Istanbul Film Festival and the Nordic Light photography festival in Kristiansund, Norway, with exhibitions and film screenings. Begins to design the book *Anywhere*, incorporating photographs old and new. German student Léa Duppe writes a thesis on Klein, which becomes a book. *Contacts* is published in Italy, with several foreign-language editions.

2022 Klein dies in Paris on 10 September.

Selected bibliography

Life Is Good & Good for You in New York: Trance Witness Revels, photographs, text and design by William Klein, Paris: Editions du Seuil; Milan: Feltrinelli; London: Vista Books, 1956

Rome, photographs, text and design by William Klein, Paris: Editions du Seuil; Milan: Feltrinelli; London: Vista Books, 1958–59

Moscow, photographs, text and design by William Klein, Tokyo: Zokeisha; Milan: Silvana; New York: Crown Publishers, 1964

Tokyo, photographs, text and design by William Klein, Tokyo: Zokeisha; Milan: Silvana; Paris: Delpire éditeur; New York: Crown, 1964

Mister Freedom, screenplay, photographs by Jurgen Vollmer, Jeanne and William Klein, Paris: Éditions Eric Losfeld, 1970

New York 54/55, portfolio, introduction by Alain Jouffroy, Jean-Marc Bustamante and Bernard Saint-Genes, Paris, 1978; 12 photographs, limited edition of 50

William Klein: Photographs, text by John Heilpern, New York: Aperture, 1981

William Klein, text by Alain Jouffroy, 'I grandi fotografi' series, Milan: Fabbri, 1982

William Klein: photographe, etc., text by Carole Naggar, design by William Klein, Paris: Centre Georges Pompidou/Éditions Herscher, 1983

William Klein, text by Christian Caujolle, 'Photo Poche' series, Paris: Centre National de la Photographie, 1985; new ed. Arles: Actes Sud, 2008

William Klein, Tokyo: Pacific Press Service, 1987

The Films of William Klein, text by Bruce Jenkins and Jonathan Rosenbaum, Minneapolis: Walker Art Center, 1988

William Klein: Close-Up, London and New York: Thames & Hudson, 1989

1 città + i mondiali: Torino 90, text by Guy Mandery, Milan: Federico Motta Editore, 1990

William Klein: Films and Photography, Tokyo: Pacific Press Service, 1991

In & Out of Fashion, text by Martin Harrison, London: Jonathan Cape; New York: Random House; Paris: Éditions du Seuil; Heidelberg: Braus, 1994

Citizen Sidel, photographs by William Klein, text by Jerome Charyn, Paris: Coromandel, 1994

New York 1954–1955, text, photographs and design by William Klein, Paris: Marval; Manchester: Dewi Lewis; New York: DAP; Heidelberg: Braus; Rome: Peliti; Barcelona: Lunwerg, 1995

William Klein: Portfolio, text by Christine Claussen, Hamburg: Stern, 1997

William Klein: Films, text by Claire Clouzot, Paris: Marval; New York: Powerhouse, 1998

Reporters Sans Frontières, text by Robert Delpire and William Klein, Paris: Idéodis, 2001

Paris + Klein, text by William Klein and Anthony Lane, Paris: Marval; New York: DAP, 2003

MMV Romani, Rome: Contrasto/Fendi, 2005

William Klein: Retrospective, text by Alain Sayag and Quentin Bajac, Paris: Marval/ Centre Georges Pompidou; Rome: Contrasto; Barcelona: Lunwerg, 2005

Clichy sans cliché, Paris: Delpire éditeur, 2006

William Klein: Films and Photos, Books and Paintings, USA Greece Paris, text by Jack Lang, Thessaloniki: Thessaloniki International Film Festival, 2007

William Klein: Contacts, Rome: Constrasto; Paris: Delpire éditeur, 2008

William Klein: Paintings, Etc., text by David Campany, Rome: Constrasto, 2012

William Klein: Yes, text by David Campany, London: Thames & Hudson, 2023

Selected exhibitions

1951 Galerie Dietrich-Lou Cosyn, Brussels

1952 Piccolo Teatro, Milan; Galleria del Milione, Milan

1953 Galerie Apollo, Brussels

1954 Salon des Réalités Nouvelles, Paris; Subjektive Fotografie 2, Saarbrucken

1956 La Hune, Paris

1961 Fuji Photo Salon, Tokyo

1963 'Thirty Photographers of the Century', Photokina, Cologne

1967 Stedelijk Museum, Amsterdam

1978 Apeldoorn Museum, Apeldoorn, then touring the Netherlands; guest of honour at the Rencontres Internationales d'Arles; Photographers' Gallery, London

1979 Galerie Canon, Geneva; Fondation Nationale de la Photographie, Lyon

1980 MoMA, New York; ICP, New York

1981 Light Gallery, New York; Galerie Zabriskie, Paris; American Center, Paris; Ikona Photo Gallery, Venice

1982 Galerie Municipale, Albi, France; International Festival, Malmö; Galerie Municipale du Château d'Eau, Toulouse

1983 Centre Georges Pompidou, Paris; Galerije grada Zagreba, Zagreb

1984 Galerija Beograd, Belgrade

1985 Corcoran Gallery, Washington, DC; Galerie Zabriskie, Paris; Châteaux de la Drôme, France

1986 Victor a & Albert Museum, London; Fotofest, Houston, TX

1987 Museum of Photographic Arts, San Diego; Printemps Ginza, Tokyo; Museum of Modern Art, Paris

1988 Musée d'Elysée, Lausanne;

Cinémathèque Suisse, Lausanne; National
Museum of Art, Osaka; Ludwig Museum,
Cologne; Galerie Arena and Hôtel de Ville,
Arles

1989 Walker Art Center, Minneapolis; Finnish
Film Archives, Helsinki; Galerie Zabriskie,
Paris, Art&, Trieste and Turin; Photographers'
Gallery and Museum of the Moving Image,
London

1990 Zabriskie Gallery, New York; International
Fashion Festival, Budapest; Hasselblad
Center, Gothenburg, then touring Sweden;
Biblioteca Nazionale, Turin; Museum
Folkwang, Essen, then touring

1991 Hamiltons Gallery, London; Réverbère 2,
Intercolor, FNAC Lyon; Fondation Cartier,
Jouy-en-Josas; Exposure Gallery, Tokyo

1992 Museo de Bellas Artes, Almería;
Stadtmuseum and Mosel & Tschechow
Gallery, Munich; Howard Greenberg Gallery,
New York

1993 Printemps de la Photo, Cahors; Museum
Morsbroich, Leverkusen; film screening at
the Amphitheatre of Arles

1994 Galerie Zabriskie and FNAC, Paris;
Hamiltons Gallery, London; ICP, New
York; Fahey-Klein, Los Angeles; Supreme
Burgrave's House, Prague

1995 Museum of Modern Art, San Francisco;
FNAC, Marseille: Bayly Art Museum,
Charlottesville, VA; FNAC Étoile, Paris,
then touring

1996 Howard Greenberg Gallery, New York;
Fundación Caixa, Barcelona; Walker Art
Center, Minneapolis; Maison Européenne
de la Photographie, Paris

1997 Centre Saint-Gervais, Geneva;
Fondazione Italiana della Fotografia, Turin;
Hamiltons Gallery, London; Fundación
Caixa and FNAC, Madrid; Chapelle de
Beaune, France, as part of the Rencontres
de l'ARP; Deichtorhallen, Hamburg;
Pushkin Museum, Moscow

1998 The Manege, Moscow; FNAC, Paris;
Jackson Fine Art, Atlanta, GA; Scottish
National Gallery, Edinburgh

1999 Foire Internationale d'Art Contemporain,
Paris; Paris Photo, Carrousel du Louvre, Paris;
Nouveau Théâtre, Angers; La Passerelle, Gap,
France; Cinéma des Cinéastes, Paris; Musée
de Grenoble, Grenoble

2000 Galleria Carla Sozzani, Milan; Harvard
Art Museums, Cambridge, MA

2001 'Les années Pop', Centre Georges
Pompidou, Paris; Porto Festival, Porto;
Howard Greenberg Gallery and Charles
Cowles Gallery, New York

2002 Maison Européenne de la Photographie,
Paris; Palazzo delle Esposizioni, Rome; Paris
Photo, Carrousel du Louvre, Paris

2004 House of Photography, Moscow

2005 'Rétrospective', Centre Pompidou, Paris

2006 Maison du Danemark, Paris

2007 'Prints 1955–2007', Howard Greenberg
Gallery, New York; 'Italie double vision',
Maison Européenne de la Photographie,
Paris; Artothèque Municipale, Grenoble

2008 'Réalités', Maison Européenne de la
Photographie, Paris; 'Paris en couleurs',
Hôtel de Ville, Paris; 'Mai 68, l'exposition
historique', Galerie Cosmos, Paris

2009 Polka Galerie, Paris

2012 HackelBury Fine Art, London; 'William
Klein + Daido Moriyama', Tate Modern, London

2013 Howard Greenberg Gallery, New York;
FOAM Fotografiemuseum, Amsterdam

Films

Films by William Klein

1958 *Broadway by Light*, colour, 35 mm,
12 mins, Argos Film

1959 *How to Kill a Cadillac*, colour, 35 mm,
12 mins

1962 Five films for the news series
Cinq colonnes à la une, b&w, 16 mm,
each 15 mins, ORTF
Les Français et la politique, documentary,
never broadcast, b&w, 90 mins, ORTF, Paris

1963 *Aux Grands Magasins*, documentary
with Simone Signoret, b&w, 16 mm, 90 mins
1964–65 *Float Like A Butterfly, Sting Like
A Bee (Cassius le Grand)*, b&w, 35 mm,
100 mins, Paris, Delpire Productions, winner
of the grand prize at the Tours International
Film Festival
1965–66 *Who Are You, Polly Maggoo?*, b&w,
35 mm, 105 mins, Paris, Delpire Productions,
winner of the Jean Vigo Prize
1967 *Far From Vietnam*, collaboration with
Chris Marker, Joris Ivens, Alain Resnais,
Jean-Luc Godard and Claude Lelouch,
colour, 35 mm, 120 mins
1967–68 *Mr Freedom*, 35 mm, 100 mins,
Paris, OPERA
1969 *The Pan-African Festival of Algiers*,
colour, 35 mm, 120 mins, Algiers, ONCIC
1970 *Eldridge Cleaver, Black Panther*, colour,
35 mm, 75 mins, Algiers, ONCIC
1972 'Le Grand Café', part of the series *Les
cinéastes témoins de leur temps*, 16 mm,
60 mins, Parc Films
1974 *Muhammad Ali, the Greatest*, re-edited
version of *Float Like A Butterfly, Sting Like A
Bee*, incorporating the 1974 Ali–Foreman fight
in Zaire, b&w and colour, 35 mm, 120 mins,
Paris, Films Paris–New York
1975–76 *The Model Couple*, colour, 35 mm,
100 mins, Paris, Films Paris–New York
1977 *Hollywood, California*, colour, 16 mm,
75 mins, Munich, OKO Productions
1978 *Music City*, colour, 16 mm, 75 mins,
Munich, OKO Productions
Maydays, b&w, 16 mm 100 mins, Paris,
Films Paris–New York
1980 *The Little Richard Story*, colour, 16 mm,
90 mins, Munich, OKO Productions
1981 *The French*, colour, 16 mm, 135 mins
1984 *Slow Motion*, colour, 35 mm, 30 mins,
Paris, Musée de la Villette
1985 *Fashion in France*, colour, 35 mm,
90 mins, Kuiv Productions, Ministère
de la Culture, TFI
1986 *Contact Sheets*, b&w, 35 mm, 15 mins,

Paris, Centre National de la Photographie
1989 *Carte d'Identité, État des Lieux, Ciné
Défense, La Grande Arche*: four short films
for the exhibition 'La traversée de Paris'
1990 *Contacts*, TV series on photography
devised by William Klein, comprising
22 films to date
1991 *Babilée '91*, b&w, 16 mm, 90 mins,
Paris, Lieurac Productions
1994 *In & Cut of Fashion*, b&w and colour,
35 mm, 85 mins, Paris, Films Paris–New York
1998–99 *Messiah*, colour, 35 mm, 120 mins,
Paris, Kuiv Productions
Since 1972, William Klein has also made more
than 200 commercials for TV and cinema, for
brands including Renault, DIM and Fiat.

Films about William Klein

1963 'William Klein', part of the series *Grosse
Photographen unseres Jahrhunderts* by
L. Fritz Gruber, b&w, 30 mins, produced
by Sender Freies Berlin
1965 'William Klein', part of the series *Chambre
noire* by Claude Fayard, b&w, 36 mins,
produced by Michel Tournier, ORTF, Paris
1968 'Who Are You, William Klein?', short film
by Nicholas Garnham for the series *Release*,
colour, 30 mins, BBC
1980 'William Klein', part of the series
Les grands photographes by Catherine Ikam
and Jean-Daniel Verhaeghe, colour, 52 mins,
Antenne 2, Paris
1984 *William Klein* by Freddy Coppens,
colour, 45 mins, RTB
1991 *William Klein* by Claude Jaget, colour,
45 mins, Caméra, Lyon
1994 'William Klein' by David Brittain,
part of the series *The Late Show*, colour,
26 mins, BBC
2001 *Portrait of William Klein*, made for the
Porto Festival
2006 *William Klein*, colour, 26 mins, made for
the exhibition at the Centre Pompidou, Paris
2007 *William Klein*, 26 mins, made for
the ICP Infinity Awards